UNITED STATES POLICY
TOWARD VIETNAM, 1940-1945

United States Policy Toward Vietnam, 1940-1945

by Edward R. Drachman

Rutherford • *Madison* • *Teaneck*
FAIRLEIGH DICKINSON UNIVERSITY PRESS

To Peace and Freedom in Vietnam

CONTENTS

ACKNOWLEDGMENTS

This book grew out of research begun at the University of Pennsylvania and completed at Boston University. Many thanks are due to those persons who helped along the way: to Professors Gabriel Kolko, Hilary Conroy, and John Snell of the History Department at the University of Pennsylvania, who assisted me in my initial research and made numerous incisive comments on the manuscript; to Professor Howard Zinn of the Government Department at Boston University who offered many thoughtful and helpful suggestions; to Generals Albert C. Wedemeyer and Philip E. Gallagher, and to Colonel Stephen Nordlinger (Ret.) who unselfishly gave of their time and effort in furnishing valuable material and comments; to Mrs. Virginia Hixon, who tirelessly and cheerfully typed the manuscript; and finally to my wife Linda, whose patience, encouragement, and research assistance aided me immeasurably in completing the final copy.

INTRODUCTION

The history of the Vietnamese people is marked by their continual struggle for independence. They resisted Chinese domination for one thousand years, only to see the French gain control in 1884. For seventy years the French ruled Vietnam, and for seventy years the Vietnamese resisted.[1]

World War II afforded the Vietnamese their long-awaited opportunity to break away from France. Just as France was unprepared for the German attack at home, she was even more unprepared to resist Japanese aggression in Vietnam. When France was forced to sign the armistice with the Third Reich on June 25, 1940, the prospect of France's successfully opposing Japan's encroachments in Vietnam virtually vanished. During the war, the Japanese encouraged Vietnamese nationalism. The Vietnamese were incited by such Japanese slogans as "Asia for the Asiatics!" The Vietnamese, however, did not want to cast off French rule only to see it replaced by that of the Japanese. As a result, the Vietnamese faced the dual task of defeating the Japanese and preventing the French from reasserting control after the war.

The period between 1940 and 1945 is thus one of the most important and fascinating in the history of Vietnam. It is a period filled with great hopes and aspirations, but also with bitter disappointment and disillusionment. Pros-

---

[1] For a detailed discussion of Vietnamese resistance see Joseph Buttinger, *Vietnam: A Dragon Embattled*, 2 vols. (New York: Praeger, 1967), I, 111–226.

pects for postwar independence and peace were great, but
they rapidly faded as the French returned to try to regain
control. The result was a bitter conflict, the fruits of
which are still being reaped today.

A significant role in Vietnam's wartime and immediate
postwar period was played by the United States. This
chapter in American diplomatic history, however, is not
very well known or understood. The purpose of this book
is to analyze closely and thereby reach a greater understanding of American diplomacy in this period.

Before the start of World War II, the United States
Government had very little knowledge of or interest in
Vietnam. By 1940-1941, however, this situation changed
with dramatic suddenness. American interest in Vietnam
was aroused initially by Japan's occupation of the French
colony in 1940. The United States then began to realize
Vietnam's great strategic significance. The United States,
in fact, considered the strategic importance of Vietnam to
be so great that a conflict of interests there with Japan
became a major cause of the war between the two countries.

After the Japanese attack on Pearl Harbor and the initial Japanese conquest of Southeast Asia, the strategic
importance of Vietnam from the American military point
of view declined considerably for Allied war strategy
against Japan generally bypassed Vietnam. World War II,
however, sparked American political interest in Vietnam.
President Roosevelt was very much concerned with the
postwar future of Vietnam. He was insistent that colonialism was an important underlying cause of the war in
Asia, and he was determined to prevent France from regaining control of Vietnam. In direct opposition to France
and Britain, Roosevelt proposed that after the war Vietnam
be placed under an international trusteeship and gain independence as soon as possible. When the United States
and its allies made plans for the postwar world, however,

the United States felt compelled to abandon its trusteeship idea.

The central thesis of this book is that United States policy regarding the postwar status of Vietnam was determined primarily not by events in Vietnam itself, but by events in Europe. The United States Government maintained a "Europe first" policy which meant that Vietnam had a very low position in Washington's hierarchy of policy priorities. Washington considered more important the independence of France. A politically and economically unstable France was considered a prime target of the Soviet Union which was trying to extend rapidly its influence in Europe. The United States thus decided to support France's efforts to regain control of Vietnam in the hope that success in that venture would increase the stability and strength of the French Government.

It cannot be argued with certitude that the few American representatives in Vietnam in the fall of 1945—a Military Advisory and Assistance Group, a Military Government mission, and a handful of members of the Office of Strategic Services—could have decisively changed the course of Vietnam's history. It is possible, however, that these Americans, had they been so directed, might have been able to prevent reassertion of French control over Northern Vietnam. The policies and activities of these Americans will thus be examined very closely.

In preparing this book, I recognized three major limitations: first, lack of access to all relevant material was a major problem, as many United States Government documents dealing with this period are still classified; second, much of the material which is available is heavily biased; and third, because this period in diplomatic history is so very recent, its relevance to the current conflict may unwittingly distort rather than illuminate issues. These limitations, however, did not deter this undertaking, for as

George Kennan has noted: "The most widely neglected area in diplomatic history is the one which it is perhaps essential that we understand: namely the immediate past —the mirror of our own mistakes and achievements and the direct determinant of our current problems."[2]

    [2] George Kennan's foreword in Richard P. Stebbins (ed.), *The United States in World Affairs* (New York: Council on Foreign Relations, 1950), p. vii.

UNITED STATES POLICY
TOWARD VIETNAM, 1940-1945

1

THE UNITED STATES AND INDO-CHINA, 1940-1941

The outbreak of World War II in Europe had electrifying effects throughout the world. In Asia, the early successes of Nazi Germany were felt almost immediately. The Japanese, who for almost a decade had been warring against China, were spurred on toward further aggression and military conquest. Southeast Asia, highly prized for its strategic location and its rich reservoir of raw materials and foodstuffs, was to be their next target. The likelihood of effective resistance seemed minimal, for as the colonial powers of Europe became locked in a struggle against the German menace at home, their ability to protect their Asian colonies from Japanese encroachments steadily waned.

The Japanese quickly began to take advantage of France's rapidly deteriorating position in Europe. Japanese pressure on French Indo-China[1] increased sharply as French weakness became apparent. Long irritated by the traffic between Indo-China and China along the Hai-

[1] French Indo-China was composed of five territories: Cambodia, Laos, Cochinchina, Annam, and Tonking. Vietnam was composed of the latter three territories (Cochinchina in the south, Annam in the center, and Tonking in the north). The term Vietnam was not officially used until September 2, 1945, when Ho Chi Minh proclaimed the "Democratic Republic of Vietnam." The main concern of this book is Vietnam. In those chapters dealing with United States policy during World War II, however, I have followed the official practice of using the term Indo-China, even when referring to Vietnam specifically.

phong to Yunnan railroad which had been supplying
Chiang Kai-shek with arms and other badly needed items
for his war effort, Japan intensified its pressure on France
to shut off this flow. In April 1940, Japan had bombed the
railroad, forcing France to agree to suspension of all munitions and war materials traffic to China. The Japanese
military, however, decided they would no longer settle
for halfway measures. On June 18, 1940, one day after
France asked Germany for an armistice, Japan demanded
that France close down the railroad completely and also
allow Japan to station military observers in Indo-China
to see to it that this was satisfactorily carried out. Force
would be used if the French refused.[2] On June 20, France
reluctantly bowed to the Japanese demands.[3] This Japanese move was very significant, as Herbert Feis points out,
since it "was the first pointed threat against the European
colonial empires of the Pacific."[4]

Rendered virtually impotent in Asia after it fell to
Nazi Germany on June 25, 1940, the Vichy Government
of France decided that it was advisable to yield to increasingly bold Japanese demands. At first the Vichy regime was divided over opposition to Japan. Among those
who favored resistance were General Maxime Weygand,
the Minister of Defense,[5] and Vice Admiral Jean Decoux,
who assumed his post of Governor-General of Indo-China
on July 20, 1940. Decoux in particular advocated this

[2] *Diary of Marquis Koichi Kido,* entry for June 17, 1940. Cited by
Herbert Feis, *The Road to Pearl Harbor* (New York: Atheneum,
1965) , p. 66. Kido was Lord Keeper of the Privy Seal and one of the
most influential officials around Emperor Hirohito. An English text
of the diary was prepared for the Supreme Commander, Allied Forces,
and presented as an exhibit before the International Military Tri-
bunal of the Far East.

[3] *The Private Diaries, March 1940 to January 1941 of Paul Baudoin,* trans. Sir Charles Petrie (London: Eyre and Spottiswoode,
1948) , p. 146.

[4] Feis, *op. cit.,* pp. 66-67.

[5] General Maxime Weygand, *Memories: Rappelé au Service* (Paris:
Flammarion, 1950) , pp. 336–339.

approach, arguing that "if we must run the risk of losing Indo-China, it is better to lose it in defending it than by betraying it."[6] On August 16, however, the French Cabinet decided on nonresistance. Marshal Henri Pétain's telegram to Decoux reflected this decision:

I understand your apprehension and your anguish. It is after deep reflection that I ordered my government to open negotiations with Japan, which, by avoiding a total conflict because of Indo-China, will safeguard our essential rights. I count on you to do your best in conducting the military negotiations and to set an example of discipline to all Frenchmen.[7]

The leading proponent of Vichy's policy of nonresistance to the Japanese was Paul Baudoin, the Foreign Minister. Baudoin's views prevailed upon Pétain. Baudoin had been general manager of the Bank of Indo-China and he claimed a great knowledge of the region. Moreover, he was married to an Indo-Chinese woman. He thus had a special interest in keeping Indo-China from possible devastation by the Japanese.[8] Baudoin argued that Vichy had the following choice:

If we refuse to let the Japanese through, they will launch an attack, preceded by bombing, and we shall certainly lose the whole of Indo-China. On the other hand, if we try to come to an agreement with Japan, this will begin by recognizing our complete sovereignty over Indo-China, and we shall only partly lose the colony. It is true that the Japanese troops might remain in the country and annex it but they might also respect French sovereignty, and withdraw once the fight against Chiang Kai-shek is at an end. Between the two evils one must choose the lesser and I choose an understanding with Japan.[9]

[6] Jean Decoux, À la Barre de l' Indochine: Histoire de mon Gouvernement Général (Paris: Plon, 1952), p. 102.

[7] Ibid.

[8] See Robert Murphy, Diplomat Among Warriors (New York: Doubleday, 1964), p. 60.

[9] Baudoin, op. cit., p. 203.

On August 30, 1940, the Vichy Government signed an agreement with Japan allowing her the right of passage through Indo-China and establishment of military bases in the colony. France also recognized the predominance of Japanese economic and political interests in the Far East in exchange for Japanese recognition of French authority in Indo-China and a guarantee of the colony's territorial integrity.[10] The French were forced to sign an additional military agreement with Japan on September 22, 1940. Under the threat of an ultimatum by the Japanese that they would invade Indo-China unless France acceded to their demands, France was forced to give Japan the right to occupy Hanoi and Haiphong, and to use airfields in Tongking and to station troops there.[11] These arrangements, in effect, would allow the Japanese to complete their blockade aginst China. In another agreement, signed on July 29, 1941, joint French and Japanese defense of Indo-China was proclaimed and Japan was allowed to use military facilities throughout the colony. Finally, after Japan attacked the United States fleet at Pearl Harbor, France agreed to let Japan use all of Indo-China's economic resources in exchange for retention of her administrative powers over the colony.[12]

Concessions by France to Japan in this period were made not only because France was weak, but also because strong support was not forthcoming from the two powers that might have helped, Great Britain and the United States. Britain was preoccupied as the leader of the anti-Nazi forces in Europe and, according to Cordell Hull, at that time she "felt it impossible for her to oppose aggression in both Europe and the Far East."[13] Indeed her own

---

[10] Cordell Hull, *The Memoirs of Cordell Hull*, 2 vols. (New York: Macmillan, 1948), I, 903–904.

[11] *Ibid.*, p. 906.

[12] *Ibid.*

[13] *Ibid.*, p. 897.

weakness in Asia was revealed when in July 1940 she was forced to make a temporary concession to a Japanese demand to close the Burma Road.[14] The United States, however, was in a somewhat better position to aid France in Indo-China but chose not to do so. One of the reasons for this decision was the lack of cooperation between the United States and Britain in Southeast Asia.

The Divergence of American-British Policies in Southeast Asia from the Fall of France through the Winter of 1941

Britain realized that alone she could not possibly deter Japanese advances in Southeast Asia, but she hoped that she could do so in concert with the United States. On June 10, 1940, Lord Lothian, the British Ambassador in Washington, acting under orders from Winston Churchill, asked Secretary Hull whether the United States would confer with Britain regarding fleet movements in the Pacific and the Atlantic. Lothian was told by Hull that there probably would be no occasion for conferences in this regard.

Nonetheless, as Japan began to exert pressure on Britain to withdraw its troops from Shanghai and to close the Hong Kong frontier and the Burma Road, Britain renewed its efforts to persuade the United States to help her resist Japan. On June 27, 1940, Lothian asked Hull whether the American Secretary favored a policy toward Japan which emphasized opposition or placation. Lothian warned that if the British were forced to accede to Japan's demands, the security not only of the British Empire but also of the United States would be threatened.[15] Thus the British

---

[14] On July 17, 1940. the Japanese Foreign Minister, Hachiro Arita, and the British Ambassador to Japan, Sir Robert Craigie, signed an accord providing for a suspension of transport of all war materials, including oil and trucks, from Burma and Hong Kong into China. This suspension was to last three months. Cited by Feis, *op. cit.*, p. 71.

[15] *Ibid.*, pp. 69–70.

were appealing for American aid against Japan on what they believed was the common ground of national survival. The British proffered two general alternatives to the United States. It was hoped that Japan could be deterred either by Anglo-American pressure, in the form of an embargo or a demonstration of force by dispatching warships to Singapore, or by a mollifying offer to settle Far Eastern problems in a peaceful manner.[16]

President Roosevelt and Secretary Hull both understood Britain's plight, but they were averse to adopting either of the British proposals. On June 28, Hull told Lothian that the United States Government was opposed to an embargo and the dispatch of warships to Singapore. Hull explained further that since United States interests were not immediately involved, this country could not see how an American-sponsored placation proposal would be accepted by Japan. On the other hand, Hull stated that the United States would not object if Britain, Australia, France, and Holland themselves tried to settle with Japan by holding out economic advantages, provided these were not offered at the expense of China nor in contradiction to America's stand on principles of international conduct.[17]

The British were rebuffed once more on July 1 when Under Secretary of State Sumner Welles reaffirmed the American position. Welles argued that the United States should not use force against Japan because of the risk of war and the opposition of American public opinion, nor should she try a policy of appeasement since this would offend the American sense of justice and pride.[18]

Moreover the United States Government would continue to oppose bargaining with Japan, according to Roosevelt and Hull, since this might imply sanctioning of Japan's aggressive conduct. The United States thus concluded that

---

[16] *Ibid.*, p. 70.
[17] *Ibid.*
[18] *Ibid.*, p. 71.

any appeasement was both unnecessary and foolish, and Japan would most effectively be deterred by the threat of American retaliatory power.[19]

Thus when Hull was asked at a press conference for his opinion on Britain's closing the Burma Road, he replied that the United States was disturbed since this was an unwarranted obstruction to world trade. Moreover, Hull asserted, the United States would continue its separate and independent policy in Asia.[20] During the summer of 1940, therefore, as Feis observes, the British realized that "the United States would not share either the responsibility or risks of preventing Japan from taking what it wanted."[21]

Feis points out further that the divergence of American and British policies in Southeast Asia "was caused by the contrast in the situation of British and American peoples. One was fighting for its life, the other was not. One had an empire to lose, the other had not."[22] This divergence of policies lasted for several months. During this same period, there was also a divergence of American and French policies regarding Indo-China which must now be reviewed.

The Indo-China Problem in American-French Relations from the Fall of France through December, 1940

One of the principal objectives of the Vichy regime was the preservation of the French Empire. Vichy sought diplomatic support for this aim from two countries she

---

[19] *Ibid.*

[20] Circulated press release, printed in Department of State, *Papers Relating to the Foreign Relations of the United States, Japan: 1931–1941* (Washington: Government Printing Office, 1943) , II, 101. Cited henceforth as *Foreign Relations, Japan.* The latter part of Hull's remarks was not printed in the above release. See Feis, *op. cit.,* p. 71.

[21] Feis, *op. cit.,* p. 70.

[22] *Ibid.,* p. 71.

thought might offer it, Great Britain and the United States. Britain was quick to give support, for she too wished to preserve her empire. Vichy then concentrated on gaining support from the United States, whose position on the colonial issue was uncertain.

The formulation of United States policy toward the French Empire was complicated by the problem of deciding whether to deal with the Vichy regime under Marshall Henri Pétain or the French Committee of National Liberation under General Charles de Gaulle. On June 18, 1940, de Gaulle began to organize "Free French" forces from London. The British Gevernment gave de Gaulle considerable financial and diplomatic aid, recognizing him as the leader of all Frenchmen everywhere who wanted to fight against Germany. On September 24, 1941, the Free French National Committee was organized in London and was given a large measure of aid and recognition by the British Government. On September 26, 1941, the Soviet Union recognized de Gaulle as "chief of all the Free French." By this time, several French colonies in Africa and Asia had declared themselves behind de Gaulle.

The United States, however, unlike Britain and the Soviet Union, decided not to support de Gaulle. One reason why the United States Government decided not to establish diplomatic ties with the French Committee of National Liberation was Washington's conclusion that de Gaulle had no significant following, both inside and outside France. One year after the fall of France, for instance, William D. Leahy, United States Ambassador to Vichy, wrote to President Roosevelt:

> The de Gaulle movement has not the following indicated in the British radio news or in the American press. Frenchmen with whom I can talk, even those completely desirous of victory, have little regard for General de Gaulle.[23]

---

[23] William D. Leahy, *I Was There* (New York: McGraw-Hill, 1960), p. 462.

And Secretary Hull wrote that as late as December 12, 1942, according to his information "some 95 per cent of the entire French people are anti-Hitler, whereas more than 95 per cent of this latter number are not de-Gaullists and would not follow him."[24]

The mutual antipathy between Roosevelt and de Gaulle also influenced Washington's decision not to deal with the Committee of Liberation. The quality de Gaulle hated most in Roosevelt, according to Milton Viorst, was the President's messianism.[25] De Gaulle was incensed that Roosevelt looked upon himself as the savior of exploited peoples everywhere, and that he tried to eradicate colonialism. De Gaulle had his own sense of mission toward France and he resented Roosevelt's attempts to tell him that he knew what was best both for France and the rest of the world. According to de Gaulle,

> President Roosevelt, under cover of proclamations to the contrary, intended that French affairs should fall within his own sphere of influence, that the leading strings of our divisions should end up in his hands, and that the public powers eventually emerging from this disorder should derive from his arbitration.[26]

De Gaulle thus waged a continuous battle against Roosevelt for independence of thought and action.

Roosevelt, for his part, was disturbed because of de Gaulle's "delusions of grandeur." According to Roosevelt, France was a defeated and weak country and was not destined for glory after the war as de Gaulle claimed. Roosevelt thus saw de Gaulle as "a narrow-minded French zealot with too much ambition for his own good. . ."[27]

---

[24] Hull, op. cit., II, 1193.

[25] Milton Viorst, Hostile Allies: FDR and Charles de Gaulle (New York: Macmillan, 1965), p. 245.

[26] Charles de Gaulle, The Complete War Memoirs of Charles de Gaulle, 3 vols. (New York: Simon & Schuster, 1967), II, 385.

[27] Henry L. Stimson and McGeorge Bundy, On Active Service in Peace and War (New York: Harper, 1948), p. 546.

Roosevelt's disdain for de Gaulle was shown, for instance, at the Casablanca Conference of 1934 where Roosevelt supposedly joked about de Gaulle's references to himself first as the modern Joan of Arc and then as a current-day Clemenceau. Harry Hopkins reflected the American attitude when he reportedly mentioned to Roosevelt that de Gaulle should be allowed to play the role of Joan of Arc and the Allies should get busy and hunt up some bishops.[28]

Roosevelt was more disturbed, however, at the prospect of postwar Gaullist rule in France. Roosevelt felt de Gaulle had "some rather dubious views on democracy."[29] As the President remarked to his son Elliott:

> De Gaulle is out to achieve one-man government in France. I can't imagine a man I would distrust more. His whole Free French movement is honeycombed with police spies— he has agents spying on his own people. To him, freedom of speech means freedom from criticism . . . of him. Why, if this is the case, should anybody trust completely the forces who back de Gaulle?[30]

Roosevelt was perhaps most distressed, however, at de Gaulle's position toward the French Empire. Roosevelt, who was strongly opposed to colonialism,[31] was annoyed that de Gaulle had "made it quite clear that he expect[ed] the Allies to return all French colonies to French control immediately upon their liberation."[32]

Roosevelt's disdain for de Gaulle facilitated his decision to work with the Vichy regime. United States recognition of de Gaulle as head of a Provisional French Government

---

[28] Kenneth Pendar, *Adventures in Diplomacy* (New York: Dodd, Mead, 1945), p. 150.

[29] Stimson and Bundy, *op. cit.*

[30] Elliott Roosevelt, *As He Saw It* (New York: Duell, Sloane & Pearce, 1945), p. 73.

[31] See pp. 78–91.

[32] E. Roosevelt, *op. cit.*

was not to be given until October 23, 1944, a few months after the Allied invasion of France.

The United States policy toward Vichy was consonant with the American tradition of recognizing a government regardless of its ideological or governmental form, provided that it conducted its international relations peacefully and carried out its international obligations. Robert Murphy argues that, contrary to the impression left by William L. Langer,[33] American policy toward France did not involve a choice of alternatives. According to Murphy,

> Our Embassy was not conscious of having any choice. . . . We found ourselves there in [Vichy] in the summer of 1940 because our diplomats had automatically followed the French Government to Vichy just as they had followed it at first to Tours and then to Bordeaux. Nobody questioned the legality of the French Government which finally settled in Vichy. . . . Our relations with Vichy . . . never were a "gamble." At all times we had much to win and we never risked a substantial loss. . . .[34]

The United States Government hoped that its Vichy policy would yield many advantages. First, Washington felt that maintaining relations with Vichy was the most effective way to prevent France from further aiding the Nazi war effort, especially in North Africa and the Middle East. Murphy was hopeful that Washington could work with French military leaders, General Maxime Weygand in particular, to prevent German occupation of French possessions in these two areas.[35] A second important consideration was that representatives of the United States Government in France had known the politicians and military leaders in the Vichy Government for many years and considered their cooperation essential for intelligence

---

[33] William L. Langer, *Our Vichy Gamble* (New York: Norton, 1966).
[34] Murphy, *op. cit.*, p. 65.
[35] *Ibid.*, p. 68.

purposes. Thus "it would have been idiotic to cut ourselves off from this vital spring of information."[36] Winston Churchill noted the success of the United States Vichy policy when he proclaimed in the House of Commons, on December 10, 1942, that it "gave us a window on that courtyard which otherwise would not have existed."[37]

In the early years of Washington's diplomacy with Vichy, one of the main concerns of the United States Government was the mobilization of French resistance against the Axis powers wherever and whenever possible. Of particular importance to the United States in this regard was the situation in Indo-China. According to the United States Government, success in halting Japanese aggression in Southeast Asia to a great degree depended on whether Japan could be stopped from taking over Indo-China.

After Japan made its first major demand regarding Indo-China on June 18, 1940, France delayed her response, for she hoped to counter with a display of diplomatic and military force. She realized that Britain probably would not be able to help her in Asia since she had to concentrate her defenses in Europe. Thus the only effective help, according to France, had to come from the United States.

The earliest French requests for military aid and the American refusals were revealed in a memorandum of September 19, 1940, which was handed by the Vichy Government to H. Freeman Mathews, the new American chargé d'affaires at Vichy. According to this memorandum, on June 18 and 19, Court Saint-Quentin, the French Ambassador in Washington, had informed the United States Government of France's position and had asked what the United States attitude would be "in case of Japanese aggression against Indo-China." Under-Secretary Sumner Welles replied that the United States would not "enter

---

[36] Langer, *op. cit.*, p. 387.

[37] Winston S. Churchill, *The Second World War*, 6 vols. (New York: Bantam, 1961), V, 556.

into war with Japan" and therefore "could do nothing" to help the French.[38]

The first overt sign of United States displeasure with Japanese advances in Southeast Asia was indicated on July 15, 1940, just one day after Britain decided to close the Burma Road to China but about a month after a similar concession by France in Indo-China. In a public pronouncement, Secretary Hull maintained that the United States at this time was not inclined to risk war by threatening to stop Japan by force. Rather, the United States hoped that denouncing the erection of artificial barriers to world trade would be a sufficient deterrent to further Japanese aggression.[39]

Despite the evident displeasure of the United States Government, Japan continued to press France to make concessions in Indo-China. Vichy reacted by instructing Ambassador Saint-Quentin to inform the United States Government confidentially of the Japanese demands and to stress that "the resistance of the French Government to the Japanese demands would necessarily depend to a large extent on the nature and effectiveness of the support which the American Government would be disposed to give it."[40]

Washington's answer to this French request was given orally to Ambassador Saint-Quentin on August 6, 1940, by James Clement Dunn, political advisor of the State Department. Dunn explained that the United States was doing what it could "within the framework of our established policies" to stabilize the situation in the Far East and that the United States was exerting economic pres-

---

[38] "The Chargé in France (Mathews) to the Secretary of State," Vichy, September 19, 1940, in United States Department of State, *Foreign Relations of the United States, Diplomatic Papers 1940* (Washington: G.P.O., 1955), IV, The Far East, pp. 131–134.

[39] Hull, *op. cit.*, I, 901.

[40] Cited by William L. Langer and S. Everett Gleason, *The Undeclared War, 1940–1941* (New York: Harper, 1953), p. 10.

sure on Japan. Dunn pointed out that the United States fleet was now based in Hawaii and urged Saint-Quentin to learn whether France could delay discussions with the Japanese over Indo-China. Saint-Quentin replied that Dunn's response would not enable Vichy to resist the Japanese demands and that Vichy probably could not delay the negotiations. Saint-Quentin "went on to say that in his opinion the phrase 'within the framework of our established policies,' when associated with the apparent reluctance of the American Government to consider the use of military force in the Far East at this particular time, meant that the United States would not use military or naval force in support of any position which might be taken to resist the Japanese attempted aggression on Indo-China."[41] When Dunn apparently did not deny Saint-Quentin's interpretation of his remarks, Saint-Quentin reported to Vichy that it could not expect United States military aid against Japan.[42]

The refusal of the United States Government to offer military support to France to defend Indo-China was evidently an important consideration in France's decision not to resist Japanese demands in her colony. On August 17, 1940, Foreign Minister Paul Baudoin summoned Robert Murphy to inform him of new Japanese demands on Indo-China. Baudoin explained to Murphy that "in the absence of any material support from Great Britain and the United States as distinguished from the enunciation of principles," the French Government would be forced to yield to the Japanese. According to Baudoin, Murphy explained that he understood France's plight but "that in the present circumstances it would be vain to expect from the American Government anything other

---

41 From Dunn's notes, cited by Langer and Gleason, *ibid.*

42 Full text of Saint-Quentin's report cited by Francois Charles-Roux, *Cinq Mois Tragiques aux Affairs Étrangères* (Paris: Plon, 1949), pp. 251-252.

than a verbal condemnation of Japanese initiatives." Baudoin then suggested that Washington warn Japan that military occupation of Indo-China must be temporary.[43] This suggestion was forwarded to Washington. On August 21, 1940, Under Secretary Welles made the following reply to the French request:

> We understand the situation of the French Government and, since we are not in a position to come to its assistance, we do not feel that we have the right to reproach it for according military facilities to Japan. But, if we were to recommend to Tokyo that its occupation be temporary, we would be accepting the principle of it. But this would be a violation of the *status quo,* the maintenance of which we shall continue to insist upon.[44]

Although Washington was not prepared to offer France military aid, contrary the impression left by Welles on August 21, it did try to apply diplomatic pressure on Vichy to resist new Japanese demands on Indo-China. Robert Murphy recalls that he "was instructed to make one 'representation' after another to the French Government in Vichy about Japanese demands."[45] Hull asserts that he instructed the United States Embassy in Vichy on August 26, 1940 "to state to Marshal Pétain's Foreign Office that we hesitated to believe that the French Government actually had made the concession to the Japanese which was being reported to us." Hull concluded that "the making of such concessions . . . would react unfavorably on American public opinion."[46] The French Foreign Office replied that no agreement had yet been made with Japan, that Japan had demanded only that France let Japanese military forces pass through Indo-China, and that France

---

[43] Baudoin, *op. cit.,* pp. 203–204.
[44] Text of remark as reported by Saint-Quentin in Charles-Roux, *op. cit.,* p. 255.
[45] Murphy, *op. cit.,* p. 60.
[46] Hull, *op. cit.,* I, 903.

was insisting that there be no military occupation of the colony.[47]

The French-Japanese agreement of August 30, 1940, on the right of Japanese troop passage and bases in Indo-China did not become known in Washington until September 5. As late as September 4, Hull issued a public statement explaining that the United States was reluctant to believe the still unconfirmed reports of these Japanese demands on Indo-China. But Hull warned, however, that "should events prove these reports to have been well founded, the effect upon public opinion in the United States would be unfortunate."[48] Thus the United States seemed to hope to stop Japanese aggression by adding the threat of unfavorable American public opinion to its previous condemnation of Japanese obstruction of world trade. When the United States finally learned of France's concessions to Japan, Washington was piqued since they further upset the status quo in the Pacific, the preservation of which was a fundamental American objective until the Japanese attack on Pearl Harbor. Moreover, the United States was disappointed and annoyed that the French Government had concluded the agreement without first consulting Washington.[49] This apparent lack of

[47] *Ibid.*

[48] *Ibid.*

[49] "The Secretary of State to the Chargé in France (Mathews) at Vichy," Washington, September 9, 1940, in *Foreign Relations, The Far East, op. cit.,* pp. 104–105.

It is important to note that France insisted that she always had consulted with the United States on matters relating to Indo-China. See seven-page memorandum in defense of French policy in the Far East from June through September, 1940. Reprinted in "The Chargé in France (Mathews) to the Secretary of State," Vichy, September 19, 1940, *ibid.,* pp. 131–134. Adrienne Hytier also argues that the Vichy Government kept Washington fully informed: "The French, whose one hope was the United States, kept Washington fully informed of the developments of the Franco-Japanese crisis. Baudoin kept in touch with Murphy, Saint-Quentin communicated all his information to the State Department, Admiral Decoux . . . kept the American consul in Hanoi, Charles S. Reed, informed of what was happening on

consultation between the United States and France was indeed serious, yet the situation was to grow worse as the war progressed.

Washington was becoming further vexed by the French because of their apparent submissiveness before Japanese demands. The French, however, despite repeated scoldings from the United States, were in such a desperate position that they continued to implore the United States for military aid in defense of Indo-China. On September 24, the French Ambassador called on Under-Secretary Welles in Washington. He first informed Welles that the French in Indo-China had resisted a Japanese military invasion near Langson which had been undertaken "in complete disregard" of agreements between Vichy and Tokyo. The Ambassador hoped that this would show the American people that "the French were not as supine as they had recently been made to appear." The Ambassador then asked whether the United States Government could "give some assurance that the Indo-Chinese Government could obtain munitions and aviation matériel in the United States." Welles replied that "as a matter of policy" the United States would furnish material assistance to "the victims of aggression in the Far East," but he reminded the Ambassador that at the very moment of his request for the United States to sell airplanes to Indo-China, ninety airplanes which the French Government had purchased from the United States earlier "were fast deteriorating on the hills of Martinique."

Welles observed that "this was an absurd situation." The Ambassador explained that he "had done his utmost to persuade his Government to send these airplanes to

---

the spot. Besides, Charles Arsène-Henry, the French Ambassador in Tokyo, was a close friend of Grew's. However, Washington later adopted the astonishing attitude that it had known nothing of the Franco-Japanese negotiations and that it had never directly or indirectly approved them. . . ." *Two Years of French Foreign Policy: Vichy, 1940–1942* (Paris: Librarie Minard, 1958), p. 197.

Indo-China," but "in response to his vigorous telegrams to his own Foreign Office on the subject he had received only negative replies which had, in effect, shown great irritation with him because of his insistance."[50]

Even though the United States continued to refuse France military aid for use in Indo-China, Vichy kept pressing Washington. On December 11, the French Ambassador once again called on Welles to ask for this aid. Welles bluntly refused to offer any American assistance. The Ambassador accepted this news without objection, but then read to Welles a telegram which he had received from Admiral Jean Decoux, the Governor-General in Indo-China, urging that the United States be asked to sell Indo-China the ten airplanes which had been destined for Thailand but which had been delayed in the Philippines. Welles told the Ambassador that "there could be no question of sending these airplanes to Indo-China," since they were to be used by the United States Army, and any spare airplanes would in any case be sold to China. Welles then repeated his amazement that the French Government "would continue to permit the 100 new military planes purchased in the United States to go to pieces in Martinique when these planes would be of enormous value to Indo-China in resisting aggression. . . ."

Welles then reported what appeared to be a growing subservience of Vichy to Germany. The French Ambassador, upon hearing Welle's argument about the planes in Martinique, "thereupon burst into a state bordering upon frenzy." He "shouted" to Welles that he had sent ten telegrams to Vichy insisting that the terms of the armistice allowed for shipment to Indo-China of the planes in Martinique, and that "each time he had been turned down flatly" on the grounds that "the armistice would not

---

[50] "Memorandum of Conversation by the Under-Secretary of State (Welles)," Washington, September 24, 1940, *Foreign Relations, The Far East, op. cit.,* pp. 146–147.

permit." The Ambassador concluded, however, that he was just informed that Pierre Laval was "taking a contrary view" and he hoped that the planes in Martinique would soon be shipped to Indo-China.[51]

Further French efforts to influence the United States to send France military aid were made in Indo-China through the United States Consul at Hanoi. On December 19, the United States Consul cabled Secretary Hull that Admiral Jean Decoux had told him that most Frenchmen in Indo-China would resist further Japanese aggression, but "without material aissistance, especially airplanes, Indo-China could not long resist. . . ."[52] The United States Government, however, refused to give the aid which Decoux requested.

United States policy regarding Indo-China from the fall of France until December 1940 can now be summarized. Washington did not feel that a Japanese military attack on Indo-China was imminent. Thus it encouraged Indo-China "to delay and parley, and hold out to the last minute against Japanese demands."[53] The United States believed that this policy had several advantages: first, the United States hoped to gain time to prepare itself for a possible military encounter with Japan which might arise in the near future;[54] second, delaying tactics would give the United States time to aid Britain, so Washington would have a stronger ally in case it too became involved in hostilities; and third, to help Britain effectively, a war in both Europe and Asia had to be avoided.

Instead of reacting forcefully to Japanese encroachments in Indo-China, the United States chose verbal condem-

---

[51] "Memorandum of Conversation by the Under-Secretary of State (Welles) ," Washington, December 11, 1940, *Foreign Relations, The Far East, op. cit.*, pp. 232–233.

[52] "The Consul at Hanoi (Reed) to the Secretary of State," Hanoi, December 19, 1940, *ibid.*, pp. 243–244.

[53] Hull, *op. cit.*, I, 906.

[54] *Ibid.*, p. 916.

nation. Japan was thus chastised for obstructing world trade, inflaming American public opinion, and upsetting peaceful international relations. Thus American policy toward Indo-China continued the interwar Far East policy which, from the Washington Disarmanment Conference of 1922, had extended the diplomatic frontier of the United States beyond its military frontier and had relied on what Professor John Fairbank has called "paper policies" which were not backed up by force.[55]

As the United States in the spring of 1941 began to perceive the threat which Japanese advances in Indo-China posed to her own interests in the Pacific, however, her policies underwent an important change. Henceforth Japan would have to be shown—short of war—that the United States was determined to prevent further Japanese aggression in Southeast Asia.

The Indo-China Problem in United States Policy from the Spring of 1941 to Pearl Harbor

By the spring of 1941, the Japanese decided that the occupation of south Indo-China was an "urgent matter." In this area there was strong anti-Japanese sentiment which was resulting in economic disadvantages for Japan. Rice exports from Indo-China to Japan were decreasing and Japan feared that vital Indo-Chinese resources, such as rubber, tin, coal, and manganese might be diverted to other markets.[56]

On June 11, 1941, Japan decided to accelerate her advances into Southeast Asia. Japan wanted to secure an agreement with French Indo-China to provide for Japa-

[55] For further discussion of this problem, see John K. Fairbank, *The United States and China* (New York: Viking, 1958), p. 9.

[56] Louis Morton, *Strategy and Command: The First Two Years* (Washington: Department of the Army, 1962), p. 64.

nese military occupation of the southern part of that country.

> The use of force was precisely stipulated: if French Indo-China resisted, Japan would resort to arms; if America, Britain, and the Netherlands attempted to interfere, and if no other solution were possible, Japan would 'not avoid risking' an all-out war.[57]

After a discussion of this new policy on June 11, 12, and 16, Japan concluded that she "would deal decisively with anyone who tried to stand in her way."[58] Finally, on June 22, this plan was sanctioned by the Emperor.

On the same day, German forces invaded the Soviet Union. Japanese leaders were divided as to what course Japan should follow. One group, led by Foreign Minister Yosuke Matsuoka, urged that Japan should also attack the Soviet Union. The dominant Army and Navy leaders, however, argued that Japan should not attack the Soviet Union because Japan was not prepared for such a military undertaking and because Japan, after Germany defeated the Soviet Union, would probably be able to secure gains from this victory without fighting herself. This latter view prevailed, mainly because key officers in the Japanese War Ministry wanted Japan to move southward first to occupy southern Indo-China and establish closer military ties with Thailand. Japanese military movements northward would have to await more favorable circumstances.[59]

At an imperial conference on July 2, Japan decided to concentrate on successfully concluding the war in China and at the same time to advance south. Japan hoped to avoid war with Britain and the United States, but "in order

---

[57] Robert C. Butow, *Tojo and the Coming of the War* (Princeton, N.J., Princeton University Press, 1961), p. 210. The documentation in this citation as well as throughout much of the book is from official Japanese sources.

[58] *Ibid.*

[59] *Ibid.*, p. 214.

to achieve her objectives" in the south, Japan would "not decline a war with England and the United States." In other words, as Butow explains, "Japan would be ready to use force against anyone who cut across the bow of her driving ambition."[60]

This decision by Japan signaled an important turn in Japanese-American relations. Japan began to intensify her demand to control all Indo-China. This Japanese demand on Indo-China increased the awareness of the United States Government of the danger of Japanese advances in Indo-China. Earlier in March 1941, in anticipation of increased Japanese pressure on Indo-China, the United States had entered into a strategic accord with Britain. According to this agreement, the United States would aid in the British military effort in the Far East, but she would give Britain no explicit guarantee and would not go so far as to pledge to go to war against Japan if Britain judged such a decision necessary.[61] Now on July 21, 1941, the first major report to President Roosevelt on the strategic significance of Indo-China to United States security, made by the Navy Department, foreshadowed further American commitment. The report read, in part, as follows:

> The occupation of Indo-China by Japan is particularly important for the defense of the United States, since it might threaten the British position in Singapore and the Dutch position in the Netherlands East Indies. Were they to pass out of their present control, a very severe blow

---

[60] *Ibid.*, p. 219.

[61] For further information and analysis of the American commitment to Britain in the Far East in the years 1940–1941, see *Pearl Harbor Attack*, Hearings before the Joint Committee on the Investigation of the Pearl Harbor Attack, U.S. Congress, 79th Cong., 1st Sess., Washington, 1946, part 15, pp. 1485–1550. Cited henceforth as *Pearl Harbor Attack*. See also Feis, *op. cit.*, pp. 167–168, and Raymond A. Esthus, "President Roosevelt's Commitment to Britain to Intervene in a Pacific War," *The Mississippi Valley Historical Review*, L (June, 1963), pp. 28–38.

would be struck at the integrity of the defense of the British Isles, and these Isles might well be overcome by the Germans. It can thus be seen what a very close interest, from a military viewpoint, the United States has in sustaining the *status quo* in the southern portion of the Far East.[62]

After Vichy acceded to the Japanese demands to maintain troops and to establish air and naval bases in southern Indo-China, the Japanese Ambassador to Washington, on July 23, 1941, informed Acting Secretary of State Welles that assurance was needed that rice, raw materials, and other foodstuffs would be allowed to flow uninterruptedly to Japan. The Ambassador further explained that Japan had to take this step in Indo-China as a safeguard against a policy of encirclement which she felt certain other powers were plotting. Welles, reflecting both the disapproval and apprehension of the United States Government, made the following points in his reply:

1. The Vichy agreement with Japan was obviously made under pressure from Germany and thus was designed to aid Germany's policy of world domination and conquest.

2. The conclusion of an agreement being discussed by Secretary Hull and the Japanese Ambassador promised to bring Japan much more economic security than she could gain by occupation of Indo-China.

3. United States policy was not to encircle Japan, nor was it designed to pose a threat to her security.

4. Great Britain also was not a threat to Japan, and together with the British Dominions, China, and the Netherlands, she could be expected to join with the United States and Japan in support of an American-

---

[62] "The Director of the War Plans Division of the Navy Department (Rear Admiral Turner) to the Chief of Naval Operations (Admiral Stark)," Washington, July 21, 1941, transmitted to President Roosevelt and Secretary Hull by Admiral Stark, in *Foreign Relations, Japan, op. cit.,* II, 516–520.

Japanese stand on principles of international conduct.
5. The United States must conclude that Japan was bent on a policy of expansion and conquest in Southeast Asia, and thus could see no further basis for continuing discussions between Hull and the Japanese Ambassador.[63]

On the following day, July 24, Welles informed the press of the essence of this meeting with the Japanese Ambassador. Welles stressed that Japan, in effect, was serving notice that it would pursue its aims by force or threat of force; that Japanese occupation of Indo-China could not be rationalized or justified on the basis of self-defense; that neither the United States, Great Britain, nor the Netherlands had any territorial designs on Indo-China and that these countries were not planning to threaten Japan; that the Japanese action would jeopardize the ability of the United States to procure essential raw materials, such as tin and rubber; and that Japan's steps endangered adjacent areas in the Pacific, particularly the Philippines. Therefore the United States must conclude, Welles explained, that Japan had made its move against Indo-China in order to use that colony as a springboard for further aggression in Southeast Asia and the Pacific.[64]

On the afternoon of that same day, July 24, 1941, President Roosevelt met with the Japanese Ambassador and informed him that Japan's latest move into Indo-China was viewed as a very serious matter by the United States. Roosevelt told the Ambassador forthrightly that he believed that the occupation of Indo-China "was being undertaken by Japan for the purpose of further offense."

---

[63] Department of State, *Peace and War: United States Foreign Policy, 1931-1941*, Washington, July 1, 1943, Doc. 218, "Memorandum by the Acting Secretary of State (Welles) Regarding a Conversation with the Japanese Ambassador (Nomura)", Washington, July 23, 1941, pp. 693-697. Cited henceforth as *Peace and War*.

[64] Doc. 219, "Statement by the Acting Secretary of State (Welles)," July 24, 1941, *ibid.*, pp. 698-699.

The President then proposed that if Japan would not occupy Indo-China, or would withdraw its forces of occupation which might already be there, he would do all he could to persuade China, Great Britain, and the Netherlands to join with the United States in declaring Indo-China a *neutralized area,* provided of course, Japan would also honor a similar commitment. By neutralization, Roosevelt meant that the concerned powers would not undertake any military act of aggression against Indo-China and that they would not exercise any military control over that colony. Roosevelt would try to secure a guarantee by the concerned powers that as long as the situation remained as it was, France would retain control over Indo-China. According to Roosevelt, therefore, Japan would be assured that no power would threaten her and that she could maintain access to food supplies and raw materials.

The President then addressed himself to the problem of continued shipment of oil by the United States to Japan. The Japanese Ambassador was told that the United States was keeping open this flow of oil in order to prevent Japan from seizing the Netherlands East Indies under the pretext of needed additional oil supplies. Roosevelt warned the Ambassador that if Japan tried to take the Netherlands East Indies by force, the Netherlands, with Britain's aid, would obviously resist and war would result. Since United States policy then was to assist Britain, Roosevelt warned that "an exceedingly serious situation would immediately result."[65]

The Japanese disregarded Roosevelt's remonstrations and on July 24 boldly moved into southern Indo-China. The United States Government stressed that this Japanese action "was unmistakably an overt and flagrant act of aggression."[66] As General George C. Marshall explained, this

---

[65] Doc. 220, "Memorandum by the Acting Secretary of State (Welles)," Washington, July 24, 1941, *ibid.,* pp. 699–703.
[66] Department of State, *Peace and War, op. cit.,* p. 126.

"aggression . . . gave unmistakable evidence of Japan's plan to enlarge her empire at the expense of weaker countries."[67] Japan, according to the State Department, had thus

> virtually completed the encirclement of the Philippine Islands and placed its armed forces within striking distance of vital trade routes. This created a situation in which the risk of war became so great that the United States and other countries concerned were confronted no longer with the question of avoiding such risk but from then on with the problem of preventing a complete undermining of their security. . . .[68]

On July 26, 1941, Ambassador Grew in Japan was informed by the Japanese Minister of Foreign Affairs that Vichy had consented to admit Japan to a joint protectorate of Indo-China. "This meant," according to historian Samuel Eliot Morison, "that Japan was free to extend her military occupation over the entire colony, which was done forthwith. It also completed the left curve of a strategic horseshoe around the Philippines."[69]

On the same day, July 26, President Roosevelt issued an Executive Order freezing Japanese assets in the United States which, in effect, was to stop completely trade between the United States and Japan.[70] Japanese forces, however, ignored this American action and continued to move into southern Indo-China.

President Roosevelt, in the meantime, received no reply to his neutralization proposal until August 6, when the Japanese Ambassador presented a counterproposal. The Japanese Government would not station troops in the

---

[67] Cited by Walter Millis (ed.), *The War Reports* (Philadelphia: Lippincott, 1947), p. 64.

[68] Department of State, *Peace and War, op. cit.,* p. 127.

[69] Samuel Eliot Morison, *History of United States Naval Operations in World War II,* Vol. III: *The Rising Sun in the Pacific, 1931–April 1942* (Boston: Little, Brown, 1948), p. 62.

[70] Doc. 222, "Statement Issued by the White House on July 26, 1941," Department of State, *Peace and War, op. cit.,* pp. 704–705.

southwestern Pacific areas except for Indo-China, would withdraw its troops already in Indo-China after settlement of the "China incident," would guarantee the neutrality of the Philippines "at an opportune time," and would cooperate with the United States in the production and procurement of natural resources which the United States required.

The United States, according to this counterproposal, was asked to suspend its "military measures" in the southwest Pacific areas and to advise Great Britain and the Netherlands to do the same, to cooperate with Japan in the production and procurement of natural resources required by Japan in the southwestern Pacific area, to begin working for the resumption of normal trade relations between the United States and Japan, to use its "good offices" to initiate direct negotiations between Japan and China in order to obtain a quick settlement of the China incident, and to recognize a special status for Japan in French Indo-China, even after Japan would withdraw its troops from the colony. The Japanese Ambassador further explained that Japanese occupation of Indo-China was necessary "to prevent from getting beyond control the Japanese public opinion which had been dangerously aroused because of the successive measures taken by the United States, Great Britain, and the Netherlands East Indies against Japan."[71] Japan was thus arguing the old story of preventive imperialism: she had to occupy Indo-China to prevent that territory's future use by other powers as a base for aggression against her.

The United States reaction was swift and sharp. On August 8, 1941, Secretary Hull handed the Japanese Ambassador a document which asserted that the August 6 proposal by the Japanese Government was "lacking in

[71] Doc. 223, "Oral Statement Handed by the Japanese Ambassador (Nomura) to the Secretary of State on August 6, 1941," Department of State, *Peace and War, op. cit.,* pp. 705–706.

responsiveness" to the neutralization suggestion made by President Roosevelt.[72] Furthermore, the United States, spurred by Japanese advances in Indo-China, began to cooperate more closely with Britain in Asia. In a conference during the second week in August, President Roosevelt and Prime Minister Churchill discussed the situation in the Far East. The two parties agreed to take parallel action in warning Japan against new moves of aggression. They admonished Japan that "any further encroachments . . . in the southwestern Pacific would produce a situation which would compel their governments to take counter-measures even though these might lead to war." They also agreed that the United States should continue its conversations with Japan to try to influence her to adopt a peaceful alternative course.[73]

The next step by the United States was taken on August 16. Hull told the Japanese Ambassador that the Japanese establishment of military bases in Indo-China "would mean about the last step prior to a serious invasion of the South Sea area . . . [which] would be a serious menace to British success in Europe and hence to the safety of the Western Hemisphere, including the United States." Hull thus warned that "this Government could not for a moment remain silent in the face of such a threat, especially if it should be carried forward to any further extent."[74] Moreover on the next day, President Roosevelt and Secretary Hull, after conferring with the Japanese Ambassador, handed him a document which warned that the United States considered Japanese occupation of Indo-

---

[72] Doc. 225, "Document Handed by the Secretary of State to the Japanese Ambassador (Nomura)," Washington, August 8, 1941, *ibid.*, pp. 709–710.

[73] *Ibid.*, p. 129. See also Sumner Welles' Notes on the Atlantic Conference, printed in *Pearl Harbor Attack, op. cit.*, Part 4, pp. 1784–1792.

[74] "Memorandum by the Secretary of State," Washington, August 16, 1941, in Department of State, *Foreign Relations, Japan, op. cit.*, II, 553.

China a serious threat to its security and that any further aggression might mean the proverbial last straw.[75]

Japan was in general unresponsive to American arguments. On November 20, however, Japan presented an important five point proposal to the United States. The first two points dealt directly with Indo-China:

> 1. Both the Governments of Japan and the United States undertake not to make any armed advancement into any of the regions in the Southeastern Asia and Southern Pacific area excepting the part of French Indo-China where the Japanese troops are stationed at present.
> 2. The Japanese Government undertakes to withdraw its troops now stationed in French Indo-China upon either the restoration of peace between Japan and China or the establishment of an equitable peace in the Pacific area.
> In the meantime the Government of Japan declares that it is prepared to remove its troops now stationed in the southern part of French Indo-China to the northern part of the said territory upon the conclusion of the present arrangement which shall later be embodied in the final agreement.

The United States was asked to cooperate in "securing the acquisition of those goods and commodities which the two countries need in Netherlands East Indies; . . . to restore . . . commercial relations to those prevailing prior to the freezing of the assets; . . ." to "supply Japan a required quantity of oil; . . . [and] to undertake to refrain from such measures and actions as will be prejudicial to the endeavors for restoration of general peace between Japan and China."[76]

The State Department interpreted this proposal as an unrealistic ultimatum, stressing that its acceptance would be tantamount to condoning and yielding to Japanese imperialism. Two days later, on November 22, in a conversation with Japanese Ambassadors Nomura and Kurusu,

---

[75] Department of State, *Peace and War, op. cit.,* p. 129.

[76] "Draft Proposal, Nomura to Hull," November 20, 1941, Department of State, *Foreign Relations, Japan,* II, *op. cit.,* pp. 755–756.

Secretary Hull rejected an added Japanese offer to withdraw its troops from Indo-China "after the settlement of
the China affair." Instead Hull warned that "uneasiness
would prevail as long as the troops remained in Indo-China
. . . [and] that they should get out of Indo-China."[77] And
in another conversation among these three persons on
November 26, Hull explained that "we are primarily out
for our permanent futures, and the question of Japanese
troops in Indo-China affects our direct interests."[78]

On this same day, November 26, Hull handed Nomura
a document which outlined a proposed basis for agreement
between the United States and Japan. The two Governments, according to this document, should

> endeavor to conclude among the American, British, Chi-
> nese, Japanese, the Netherlands and Thai Governments
> an agreement whereunder each of the Governments would
> pledge itself to respect the territorial integrity of French
> Indo-China and, in the event that there should develop a
> threat to the territorial integrity of Indo-China, to enter
> into immediate consultation with a view to taking such
> measures as may be deemed necessary and advisable to
> meet the threat in question. Such agreement would pro-
> vide also that each of the Governments party to the agree-
> ment would not seek or accept preferential treatment in
> its trade or economic relations with Indo-China and would
> use its influence to obtain for each of the signatories equal-
> ity of treatment in trade and commerce with French Indo-
> China.

The document also called for the withdrawal of "all military, naval, air and police forces from China and Indo-
China."[79] This United States proposal was similar in con-

---

[77] "Memorandum of a Conversation" between Nomura, Kurusu,
and Hull, Washington, November 22, 1941, in Department of State,
Foreign Relations, Japan, op. cit., II, 760.

[78] "Memorandum of a Conversation" between Nomura, Kurusu,
and Hull, Washington, November 26, 1941, *ibid.,* p. 765.

[79] "Document Handed by the Secretary of State to the Japanese
Ambassador (Nomura) on November 26, 1941," *ibid.,* pp. 768–770.

tent, although perhaps not in tone and sense of urgency, to the earlier Hay Open Door proposals regarding China. Unfortunately, however, the results of this new proposal would prove to be less effective than those of the Hay notes. Thus the United States, through its proposal on Indo-China, was continuing to rely unsuccessfully on the combination of the threat of military force and moralistic-legislative pressure as a deterrent to Japanese aggression.[80]

Several days later, on December 1, Secretary Hull rejected the earlier Japanese offer of November 20, explaining to Nomura and Kurusu that the presence of Japanese troops in Indo-China "constitutes a menace to the South Sea area, irrespective of where in Indo-China the troops are stationed." Hull then played upon what he hoped would be a Japanese fear of being jilted by Germany, explaining that Japanese troops in Indo-China made it necessary for the United States and its friends "to keep large numbers of armed forces immobilized in East Asia, and in this way Japan's acts were having the effect of aiding Hitler." Hull then concluded that the United States "could not sit still while such developments were taking place."[81]

That America's relations with Japan were rapidly deteriorating over the Indo-China issue was clearly seen in a message from President Roosevelt handed to Ambassador Kurusu by Under Secretary Welles on December 2. The message stated that Japanese military occupation of Indo-China "would seem to imply the utilization of these forces by Japan for purposes of further aggression, since no such number of forces could possibly be required for the policing of that region." The message continued that such ag-

---

[80] For a lucid discussion of the moralistic-legalistic basis of American foreign policy, see George F. Kennan, *American Diplomacy, 1900–1950* (New York: Mentor, 1963).

[81] "Memorandum of a Conversation" between Nomura, Kurusu, and Hull, December 1, 1941, in Department of State, *Foreign Relations, Japan, op. cit.,* II, 772–777.

gression might be not only against Burma, Malaya, the Netherlands East Indies, and Thailand, but also against the Philippines. The message then asked what the reasons for Japanese actions in Indo-China were and what Japanese policy in that colony actually was. Roosevelt concluded that the United States, disturbed over Germany's increasing truculence and aggression, was afraid that Japan was following the same path.

Ambassador Kurusu replied that he "could not speak authoritatively" on Roosevelt's message but he would refer it directly to Tokyo. He then reiterated Japan's previous claim that its offer to transfer all its forces from southern Indo-China to northern Indo-China meant that "it was obvious no threat against the United States was intended." Welles stressed, however, that Japan must surely be aware that the United States "has not had any aggressive intention against Japan." But Kurusu pointed out that

> the Japanese people believe that economic measures [particularly the freezing of Japan's assets in the United States] are a much more effective weapon of war than military measures; that they believe they are being placed under severe pressure by the United States to yield to the American position; and that it is preferable to fight than to yield to pressure.

Kurusu added that "wise statesmanship was needed" to reach an agreement to prevent the outbreak of war.[82]

On December 5, Hull again had a dispute with the Japanese Ambassadors as to whether the stationing of troops in northern Indo-China was for offensive or defensive purposes.[83] The same day, Nomura told Hull that

---

[82] Doc. 262, "Memorandum Regarding a Conversation between the Under Secretary of State (Welles), the Japanese Ambassador (Nomura), and Mr. Kurusu," Department of State, *Peace and War, op. cit.*, pp. 823–825.

[83] "Memorandum of a Conversation" between Nomura, Kurusu, and Hull, Washington, December 5, 1941, Department of State, *Foreign Relations, Japan, op. cit.*, II, 781–783.

Japanese troop movements along the northern frontier of Indo-China had been reinforced mainly for "precautionary" reasons. Then in an attempt to allay the fears of the United States, Nomura added:

> It seems that an exaggerated report has been made of these movements. It should be added that no measure has been taken on the part of the Japanese Government that may transgress the stipulation of the Protocol of Joint Defense between Japan and France.[84]

These remarks did not satisfy President Roosevelt who, on December 6, sent a personal message to Emperor Hirohito himself. Roosevelt decried Japanese troop movements in Indo-China as offensive in character and as detrimental to hopes for peace. He then added: "It is clear that a continuance of such a situation is unthinkable." In essence this was an ultimatum, but it was very weak since it did not carry with it any threat of force. Instead Roosevelt appealed to Hirohito's reason, sense of humanity, and "sacred duty to restore traditional amity and prevent further death and destruction in the world."[85]

This message, unfortunately, was to fall upon deaf ears, for the next day the Japanese attacked Pearl Harbor. There is no doubt that the Japanese occupation of Indo-China was the key issue of conflict between the United States and Japan which led to the attack. The United States had assessed the occupation as a serious threat to the security of the entire Pacific area, and considered this the final step, beyond which it would have to act, even if this meant war with Japan.

---

[84] "Statement Handed by the Japanese Ambassador (Nomura) to the Secretary of State on December 5, 1941," *ibid.*, p. 784.

[85] "President Roosevelt to Emperor Hirohito of Japan," Washington, December 6, 1941, *ibid.*, pp. 784–786.

2

UNITED STATES WARTIME DIPLOMACY
REGARDING THE POSTWAR
STATUS OF INDO-CHINA

One of the most important diplomatic problems the United States Government faced during the war was the determination of its policy toward the French Empire. Could Washington support the Vichy regime and not support the preservation of the French Empire? What problems did the Free French pose to the United States in this regard? Finally, what proposals did the United States make at inter-Allied wartime conferences regarding the postwar future of Indo-China and to what extent were they pursued and adopted?

The United States Assures the Vichy Government that the French Empire Will Be Preserved

The first indication of possible United States Government support for the preservation of the French Empire came on August 2, 1941, when Secretary Hull commented on the July 29 agreement between France and Japan for joint defense of Indo-China. Hull hinted that the United States Government might support French efforts to preserve their Empire, depending on how effectively the French both in Vichy and the colonies resisted attempts at domination and control by the Axis powers. Hull made no binding promise to support the French Empire, but rather gave only a qualified endorsement based on military rather than political motivations.[1]

The same qualified United States willingness to recognize the French Empire was suggested in a letter from President Roosevelt to Marshal Pétain on December 7, 1941, in response to a request from Vichy. The President stressed that the continuation of France's jurisdiction and control over its colonies was "essential . . . to the vital interests of the United States." The United States would support the preservation of the French Empire, however, only "as long as French sovereign control remains in reality purely French. . . ."[2]

A stronger expression of American support for the preservation of the French Empire was given on January 23, 1942. According to Ray Atherton, Acting Chief of the Division of European Affairs, in a conversation with French Ambassador Gaston Henri-Haye about the islands of Madagascar and Réunion, Henri-Haye seemed uncertain as to the United States policy toward French colonies. Atherton thus clarified the American position by asserting that United States policy still aimed at "maintaining the integrity of the French Empire and its eventual return in full sovereignty to the French people."[3]

The next declaration to Vichy of United States support for the French Empire came as a result of requests for similar assurances from the Free French. During the war, Frenchmen were divided on many issues, but one which virtually all were united on was the preservation of their Empire. The French were a proud people who felt that

---

[1] Department of State Release No. 374, *Department of State Bulletin,* August 2, 1941, p. 87. Cited henceforth as *DSB.*

[2] For complete text of letter, see U.S. Department of State, *Foreign Relations of the United States, Diplomatic Papers 1941, Europe* (Washington: G.P.O., 1959) , p. 205.

[3] "Memorandum of Conversation by the Acting Chief of the Division of European Affairs (Atherton) ," January 23, 1942, in U.S. Dept. of State, *Foreign Relations of the United States, Diplomatic Papers 1942, Europe* (Washington: G.P.O. 1942) , p. 687.

through their Empire they were rightfully and honorably fulfilling their *mission civilisatrice*. Perhaps no Frenchman was more distressed by the possibility that France might lose her Empire than Charles de Gaulle. To de Gaulle, France's role as a great power had not ended in France's humiliating defeat by Germany, nor would it end after the war. To de Gaulle, France had been and would continue to be a great power, not only in Europe but throughout the world.

De Gaulle considered preservation of the French Empire crucial to the maintenance of France as a great power. Throughout the war, de Gaulle made many statements regarding his determination to maintain the Empire. On June 18, 1942, for instance, de Gaulle said in London: "There is an element which, in our terrible trials, revealed itself to the Nation as essential to its future and necessary to its greatness. This element is the Empire."[4] And at the opening of the French African Conference at Brazzaville, on January 30, 1944, de Gaulle referred to the "permanent bond between France and her overseas territories."[5]

Immediately after France's fall to Germany, de Gaulle sought assurances on the French Empire from Britain and the United States. As early as June 25, 1940, he obtained from Winston Churchill a declaration which pledged that "the aim of Great Britain is the complete restoration of French territory, colonial and metropolitan."[6]

De Gaulle then concentrated on gaining similar support from the United States. In July 1941, de Gaulle sent a mission to the United States led by René Pleven. One of Pleven's most important tasks was to obtain from the

---

[4] *Free France,* July 1, 1942, p. 3.
[5] *Ibid.,* February 1, 1944, p. 122.
[6] Cited by Jean-Baptiste Duroselle, "Changes in French Foreign Policy Since 1945," in Stanley Hoffmann *et al., In Search of France* (New York: Harper & Row, 1963), p. 334.

United States Government a clear expression of support for the preservation of the French Empire.[7]

Washington virtually ignored this request until it received an urgent appeal from Thierry D'Argenlieu, the Free French Commissioner for the Pacific who was stationed in New Caledonia. Recognizing the strategic significance of this island,[8] the State Department issued a statement on March 2, 1942 designed to encourage French resistance there against the Japanese. Although the statement dealt specifically with the situation in New Caledonia, it had much wider implications. Washington gave the same qualified pledge of support for the French Empire to the Free French as to Vichy: American support would be determined by how effectively the French fought to defend their colonies. Such support, therefore, would be motivated by military considerations rather than principle.[9]

This official American response to D'Argenlieu's request disturbed Ambassador Henri-Haye, who discussed the matter three days later with Acting Secretary of State Welles. Henri-Haye explained that the United States statement on New Caledonia made it seem that the United States was dealing officially with the Free French and thus was giving them at least tacit recognition. Welles replied that he could not accept Henri-Haye's protest, but he stressed that the policy of the United States Government until then "was a policy of recognizing the right of the French people to maintain intact French territory."[10]

Welles's response evidently did not satisfy the Vichy Government, for on March 11 Ambassador Henri-Haye asked Welles outright for a public statement, "explaining

---

[7] For a discussion of the details of Pleven's mission see de Gaulle, *op. cit.,* I, 211.

[8] See Morton, *op. cit.,* p. 208.

[9] *DSB*, March 4, 1942, p. 208.

[10] "Memorandum of Conversation by the Acting Secretary of State," March 5, 1942, in U.S. Dept. of State, *Foreign Relations of the United States, Diplomatic Papers 1942, Europe, op. cit.,* p. 695.

that the United States attitude in dealing with the Free French authorities in the Pacific in no way affected its recognition of the sovereignty of France over the French possessions in the Pacific." Welles replied that the matter "would be given consideration," but that he was not authorized to say more than that.[11]

One month later, on April 12, 1942, the United States Government gave the Vichy regime an explicit assertion of support for the French Empire. The previous qualifications were now dropped. In a letter to Ambassador Henri-Haye, Acting Secretary of State Welles wrote that "the Government of the United States recognizes the sovereign jurisdiction of the people of France over the territory of France and over French possessions overseas," and "fervently hopes that it may see the reestablishment of the independence of France and of the integrity of French territory."[12]

Finally, in the fall of 1942, the Vichy Government obtained further United States support for the preservation of the French Empire. The occasion for this support was the imminent Allied invasion of North Africa. In order to enlist French support for this operation, the United States considered it a diplomatic necessity to assure France that she would back French efforts to maintain their Empire. This American assurance was communicated to Vichy in Robert Murphy's letter of November 2, 1942, to General Henri Giraud. Murphy felt that it was advantageous for the United States Government to work with Giraud since "we needed a well-known military leader who would be satisfied to fight the war and postpone political decisions for post-war France." Giraud had escaped to Africa by himself. He was thus under no obligation to the Nazis and

---

[11] "Memorandum of Conversation by the Acting Secretary of State," March 11, 1942, *ibid.*

[12] *DSB,* April 18, 1942, p. 33.

was free to organize French resistance.[13] Nevertheless, to encourage Giraud's support for the North African invasion which would be directed by the Americans, Murphy reiterated United States support for the preservation of the French Empire:

> Referring to the declarations made on various occasions by President Roosevelt and to the engagements already entered upon by the American Government as well as by the British Government, I am in a position to assure you that the restoration of France, in all her independence, in all her grandeur and in all the area which she possessed before the war, in Europe as well as overseas, is one of the war aims of the United Nations.
>
> It is well understood that French sovereignty should be reestablished as soon as possible over all territories, Metropolitan as well as colonial over which the French flag waved in 1939. . . .[14]

Several conclusions can now be drawn from the aforementioned American policy statements supporting the maintenance of the French Empire. First, the timing of the statements is significant. These statements were issued very early in the war when the United States Government was concerned more with the wartime than with the postwar status of French colonies. The United States was preoccupied with mobilizing French resistance to prevent any further takeover of French colonies by the Axis powers. A corollary of this objective, as pointed out earlier, was that support for the preservation of the French Empire depended largely upon the strength and effectiveness of French resistance. Thus as Japanese control over Indo-China became more extensive and more manifest, the sympathy of the United States Government for the restoration

---

[13] Robert Murphy, *Diplomat Among Warriors* (New York: Doubleday, 1964), pp. 115–116.

[14] Cited by William L Langer, *Our Vichy Gamble* (New York: Norton, 1966), p. 33.

of French sovereignty over that colony correspondingly diminished.

The assurances of United States support were for the French Empire in general, but by November 2, 1942, the United States Government had given a clear-cut assertion of support for the preservation of French control over Indo-China, for it was most certainly an area over which "the French flag waved in 1939."[15] As the war progressed many Frenchmen were quick to seize upon these general assertions of United States support for the French Empire as evidence of American support for postwar French control over Indo-China. A striking example of this was the citation of Welles's letter to Ambassador Henri-Haye of April 12, 1942, by Gaston Rueff, a member of the French Colonial Institute. Writing in the October 1944 issue of *Foreign Affairs,* Rueff argued: "The meaning of this statement is crystal clear. It applies without ambiguity to French Indo-China, which both technically and in practice was and is, considered a French possession."[16]

Although the United States Government in 1942 gave Vichy assurances of support for the preservation of the French Empire, the credibility of these assurances was weakened by the parallel development of an American policy of anti-colonialism, which was to grow stronger as the war progressed.

United States Opposition to Colonialism Strains the American-British-French Alliance

The opposition of the United States Government to the preservation of European empires in Asia was rooted in the traditional American antipathy to colonialism. The American Declaration of Independence was based on the

---

[15] See Murphy to Giraud as quoted above on p. 39.
[16] Gaston Rueff, "The Future of French Indochina," *Foreign Affairs,* XIII (October 1944), p. 140.

ideas of equality to all men and their right to govern themselves free from foreign control and influence. Thus the
basic idea of imperialism, i.e., the control of one state by
another presumably against the former's will, has generally been anathema to Americans.

During the early years of the war, United States encouragement of the independence of colonial areas was
reflected in numerous official pronouncements. On March
15, 1941, for instance, in an address to the White House
Correspondents Association, President Roosevelt asserted:

> There has never been, there isn't now, and there never will
> be, any race of people on earth fit to serve as masters of
> their fellow men. . . . We believe that any nationality, no
> matter how small, has the inherent right to its own na-
> tionhood.[17]

Roosevelt's position was again expressed a few months
later in the Atlantic Charter, in which the United States
and Britain stated general postwar objectives based upon
moral principles, one of which was the right of all peoples
for self-determination.

Despite this joint declaration of common goals, it soon
became clear that Roosevelt and Churchill had different
interpretations of the Atlantic Charter, particularly its
application to British and French colonies. The first open
sign of this disagreement was an exchange of views between Roosevelt and Churchill over the status of India
in March, 1942. In a letter to Churchill on March 11, 1942,
Roosevelt urged Churchill to promote self-government
for India, modelled perhaps upon the American experience
of the Ariticles of Confederation.[18] A few weeks later, on
April 12, Roosevelt expanded on his views on British
control of India in a letter to Harry Hopkins.[19] Churchill

---

[17] Cited by Samuel I. Rosenman (ed.) , *The Public Papers of FDR*
(New York: Harper, 1950) , X, 69.

[18] See Churchill, *op. cit.,* IV, 184–185.

[19] *Ibid.,* pp. 189–190.

considered Roosevelt's position ridiculous, and his response was icy.[20]

Roosevelt's anticolonial position was shared by many other important Americans both inside and outside the government. Vice President Henry Wallace and Wendell Willkie, the Republican presidential candidate defeated by Roosevelt in the election of 1940, were two of the most outspoken opponents of colonialism. Willkie, for instance, upon his return from a tour to the Far East,[21] on October 26, 1942, reported to Americans on national radio that Asians were demanding that the principles of the Atlantic Charter be applied to their region of the world. Willkie then urged the United States Government to take a stronger stand against imperialism.[22] The next day, Roosevelt was asked at a press conference for his reaction to Willkie's statements. In an effort to dispel any doubts on the American interpretation of the Charter, Roosevelt replied: "I have already made it perfectly clear that we believed that the Atlantic Charter applied to all humanity. I think that is a matter of record."[23]

On November 6, Willkie made another speech in which he denounced what he described as a continuation of the "white man's burden philosophy" in the American and British attitude toward the East. He applauded Roosevelt's statement of October 27, but he sharply criticized the British position on the Atlantic Charter. It was this biting criticism which four days later prompted Churchill's famous exclamation at the Lord Mayor's dinner at Mansion House: "I have not become the King's First Minister to preside over the liquidation of the British Empire."[24]

A few days later, Roosevelt sent Under Secretary of State

---

[20] *Ibid.*, p. 190.
[21] For an account of his trip, see Wendell L. Willkie, *One World* (New York: Simon & Schuster, 1943).
[22] *New York Times,* October 27, 1942.
[23] *Ibid.*, October 28, 1942.
[24] *Ibid.*, November 11, 1942.

William Phillips to India as his personal representative, with rank of Ambassador. Before Phillips left, on November 20, he was briefed on the American position on dependent peoples. Hull reports the following:

> I said that the President and I and the entire Government earnestly favored freedom for all dependent peoples at the earliest practicable date. Our course in dealing with the Philippines, I thought, a perfect example of how a nation should treat a colony or dependency in cooperating with it to make all necessary preparations for freedom. We offered this as a strong example to all other countries and their dependencies.[25]

By the end of 1942, therefore, a certain duality of American policy toward European colonial empires was beginning to be apparent, particularly that of the French. The United States had explicitly and quietly assured both Vichy and the Free French of American support for the preservation of the French Empire, yet at the same time had more generally and publicly proclaimed her opposition to colonialism. Roosevelt was becoming insistent, however, that the European colonial powers should follow the example set by the United States in the Philippines and begin to prepare their colonies for self-government and ultimate independence. The tentative stand which President Roosevelt was about to take against the preservation of postwar French control over Indo-China thus must be seen in the context of the general anti-colonial position of the United States Government.

ROOSEVELT'S TRUSTEESHIP PLAN FOR INDO-CHINA.—Although Roosevelt was opposed to colonialism of all the European powers, he seemed especially opposed to postwar French control over Indo-China. Indeed as Bernard Fall points

---

[25] Cordell Hull, *The Memoirs of Cordell Hull,* 2 vols. (New York: Macmillan, 1948) II, 1491.

out, the Indo-China situation "became the scapegoat for all of America's woes in the Pacific."[26] Hull recalls that military considerations and the dislike of the submissiveness of the Vichy regime to the Japanese had increased Roosevelt's desire to see Indo-China become independent after the war. According to Hull, by 1943 Indo-China

> . . . stuck in [the President's] mind as having been the springboard for the Japanese attack on the Philippines, Malaya, and the Dutch East Indies. He could not but remember the devious conduct of the Vichy Government for granting Japan the right to station troops there without any consultation with us but with an effort to make the world believe we approved. . . .[27]

Roosevelt also felt that French misrule in Indo-China had enabled the Japanese to successfully take over the colony and thus launch further aggression in Southeast Asia. The President's strong feelings on this subject were reported by his son Elliott while en route to the Casablanca Conference in February 1943. In response to Elliott's question as to how the United States could talk about not returning France's colonies to France after the war, the President replied:

> How do they belong to France . . . ? Take Indo-China. The Japanese control that colony now; why was it a cinch for the Japanese to conquer that land? The native Indo-Chinese have been so flagrantly downtrodden that they thought to themselves: anything must be better than to live under French colonial rule! Should a land belong to France? By what logic and by what custom and by what historical rule? . . . Don't think for a moment . . . that Americans would be dying tonight if it had not been for the shortsighted greed of the French, British, and Dutch.[28]

---

[26] Bernard Fall, *The Two Vietnams,* 2d Revised edition (New York: Praeger, 1967), p. 50.

[27] Hull, *op. cit.,* II, 1595.

[28] Elliott Roosevelt, *As He Saw It* (New York: Duell, Sloane & Pearce, 1945), pp. 114–116. There is some question as to the accuracy

Since President Roosevelt believed that France's mis-rule of Indo-China was an important cause of the war in the Pacific and that colonialism of any sort was despicable, he began to consider possible alternatives to postwar French rule there. The scheme that he considered in early 1943 was for Indo-China to be placed under some form of international trusteeship.

A general trusteeship plan for dependent peoples was developed early in 1943 by the State Department. According to Hull, for several months the State Department had given "intense thought" to the subject of dependent peoples. Finally, in March 1943, a draft proposal was given to Roosevelt. It was written under the guidance of Hull by Leo Pasvolsky, Special Assistant to the Secretary of State for International Organization and Security Affairs, with the help of Green Hackworth, Legal Adviser of the State Department, and Stanley Hornbeck, the State Department's Adviser on Political Relations. The draft proposal, in general, "was an effort to implement the pledges contained in the Atlantic Charter relating to the right of all peoples to choose the form of government under which they would live."[29]

The proposal had two major facets. One facet dealt with the relatively advanced colonies which soon might be ready for independence and recommended certain specific procedures which the colonial powers might take to enable these colonies to become qualified for independence. The other facet suggested that peoples liberated from Japanese rule and unprepared for autonomy should be placed under some form of international trusteeship representing a

---

of Elliott's direct quotes from his father, particularly on the colonialism question. Most scholars, however, have concluded that Elliott was reasonably accurate. Chester Wilmot, for instance, wrote that evidence indicates "that Elliott was not an inaccurate reporter of the views his father held on the colonial question." See *The Struggle for Europe* (New York: Harper, 1953), p. 633n.

[29] Hull, *op. cit.*, II, 1235–1236.

United Nations body which would be created by the end of the war.[30]

According to Hull, this trusteeship idea was "enthusiastically concurred in by the President."[31] Roosevelt wasted little time in presenting it before the Allies. The trusteeship plan was first put forth on the inter-Allied level during a White House Conference with the British on March 27, 1943. Roosevelt told British Foreign Secretary, Anthony Eden, that the United States Government was only suggesting the proposal for the consideration of the British Government and that it was not intended to be the "final word" on the matter.[32] At this meeting, Roosevelt suggested that an international trusteeship be established for Indo-China.[33] When Secretary Welles reminded the President that the United States Government had promised the restoration of French possessions, Roosevelt replied that he thought this promise referred only to North Africa. Welles, however, reminded Roosevelt that there was no such limitation.[34] Reporting over one year later on this meeting at which he was present, John Winant, the United States Ambassador to Britain, asserted that Eden advocated the advantages of national rather than international administration. Furthermore, Winant observed that the French would be "highly sensitive about the restoration of all parts of the empire to the *status quo ante* and that the British Government [would] firmly support the French position in view of its desire for the closest possible relations with France."[35]

---

[30] For details on this proposal, see *ibid.*, p. 1234.

[31] *Ibid.*, p. 1706.

[32] *Ibid.*, p. 1234.

[33] *Ibid.*, p. 1596.

[34] E. L. Woodward, *British Foreign Policy in the Second World War* (London: H.M.S.O., 1964), p. 441.

[35] "Memorandum by the Deputy Director of the Office of European Affairs (H. Freeman Mathews)," November 2, 1944, in *Foreign Relations of the United States, Diplomatic Papers 1944, the British Commonwealth and Europe* (Washington: G.P.O., 1965), pp. 777–778.

Eden did not relay his Government's response to Roosevelt's proposal until the Quebec Conference in August 1943. Roosevelt once again submitted the draft proposal to the British, and this time Eden replied that he "frankly did not like the draft" and was especially troubled by the word "independence." Instead Eden emphasized the advantages of national rather than international trusteeship.[36] At Quebec, therefore, the issue of colonialism was left unresolved.

Despite the rebuff from the British, Roosevelt continued to push the trusteeship plan. He instructed Hull to broach this matter again at the forthcoming Conference of Foreign Ministers of the United States, Britain, the Soviet Union, and China, to be held in Moscow in October 1943. In his briefing of Hull before he left for Moscow, Roosevelt reaffirmed his support for the draft proposal on dependent peoples and stressed in particular the plan for an international trusteeship over colonies which were not yet ready for independence. Among such colonies, according to Roosevelt, were Korea and Indo-China.[37]

Roosevelt hoped that a discussion of the trusteeship plan at the Foreign Ministers Conference would pave the way for action on it at the upcoming conferences at Cairo and Tehran. At the Cairo Conference of November 22-26, 1943, Roosevelt for the first time elaborated on his trusteeship plans for Indo-China. He suggested to Chiang Kai-shek

> that Indo-China be set up under a trusteeship—have a Frenchman, one or two Indo-Chinese, and a Chinese and a Russian because they are on the coast, and maybe a

---

[36] Hull, *op. cit.*, p. 1237.

[37] *Ibid.*, p. 1305. At this briefing, Roosevelt also proposed placing certain other areas under trusteeship in order to create an internationalized string of strategic air and naval bases encircling the world. He mentioned, for instance, Hong Kong, the Bonin Islands, and the Kuriles. See William D. Leahy, *I Was There* (New York: McGraw-Hill, 1960) p. 314.

Filipino and an American—to educate them for self-government. . . .[38]

Roosevelt suggested this scheme, however, only after he had "asked Chiang point blank if he wanted Indo-China." Chiang replied: "Under no circumstances!" He then added: "It's no help to us. We don't want it. They are not Chinese. They would not assimilate into the Chinese people."[39]

If Roosevelt was making an offer of Indo-China, it was obviously at variance both with his earlier devotion to the principle of independence for all colonial peoples and with U.S. qualified recognition of the French Empire. It is possible that the suggestion was not made seriously. Subsequent evidence, however, suggests the possibility that it might have been. Henry Wallace claims that before his trip to the Far East in early 1944, he was told by Roosevelt "to inform Chiang that he proposed to see that both Hong Kong and Indo-China would be returned to China. . . ."[40] In correspondence with Bernard Fall, Wallace confirmed that he personally carried Roosevelt's statement to Chiang.[41]

At the Tehran Conference of November 28-December 1, 1943, Roosevelt discussed the trusteeship question with Marshal Stalin. Again Roosevelt brought up the specific question of Indo-China. He said that he agreed "one hun-

[38] Rosenman, op. cit., XIII, 562.

[39] Cited by General Joseph W. Stilwell from his conversation with President Roosevelt on December 6, 1943. Theodore White (ed.), The Stilwell Papers (New York: Sloane, 1948), p. 253. Edward Stettinius, Jr., confirms Stilwell's account of the exchange between Roosevelt and Chiang Kai-shek. On March 17, 1944, in a briefing by Roosevelt, the President told Stettinius of his Indo-China proposal to Chiang and Chiang's immediate refusal. See Edward Stettinius, Jr., Roosevelt and The Russians (New York: Doubleday, 1949), p. 258.

[40] Henry Wallace, Toward World Peace (New York: Reynal & Hitchcock, 1948), p. 97.

[41] Fall, op. cit., p. 467. Fall suggests that Roosevelt may have offered Indo-China to Chiang as a sop to keep China in the war (p.53).

dred per cent" with Stalin that the Allies should not shed blood to restore French rule over Indo-China, and he remarked that "after one hundred years of French rule the inhabitants were worse off than they had been before. . . ." The President also told Stalin that he had just discussed with Chiang Kai-shek the possibility of a trusteeship system "which would have the task of preparing the people for independence within a definite period of time, perhaps 20 to 30 years." The Soviet leader "completely agreed with this view."[42]

On March 17, 1944, when Roosevelt told Stettinius about his Tehran discussion with Stalin, according to Stettinius's notes "the President raised the question with Joseph Stalin who said that Indo-China should be independent but was not yet ready for self-government. He said that the idea of a trusteeship was excellent. . . ."[43] Winston Churchill, however, strongly opposed Roosevelt's trusteeship scheme for Indo-China, and when he objected Roosevelt reportedly quipped, "Now look, Winston, you are outvoted three to one."[44]

By the beginning of 1944, Roosevelt seemed to have strengthened his anti-colonialism position, particularly concerning Indo-China. It is also evident that the British then feared, in effect, a chain reaction collapse of Asian colonies if Indo-China were to gain its independence. An indication of this fear was given in a discussion between Hull and Ambassador Halifax on January 3, 1944. According to Hull, Lord Halifax came to him and remarked that he had received information from his Foreign Office that Roosevelt, at the Cairo and Tehran Conferences, had

---

[42] "Bohlen Minutes, Roosevelt-Stalin Meeting at Tehran," November 28, 1943, at Roosevelt's Quarters, Soviet Embassy, in U.S. Dept. of State, *Foreign Relations of the United States, Diplomatic Papers 1943, The Conferences at Cairo and Tehran* (Washington: G.P.O., 1961), p. 485.

[43] Cited by Stettinius, *op. cit.*, p. 238.

[44] *Ibid.*

asserted to several persons that Indo-China should be placed under an international trusteeship. Halifax said that he had heard Roosevelt make remarks like this for over a year, but it was important to know whether Roosevelt's statements represented final conclusions, especially in view of the fact that the French would soon be hearing of this.[45]

Hull told Halifax that he knew no more about the matter than Halifax. Hull added that he had heard Roosevelt make such remarks occasionally just about as Halifax had heard them, and he speculated that Roosevelt and Churchill would soon reach an agreement on this issue.[46]

On January 24, 1944, Roosevelt sent Hull the following memorandum which contained the most explicit and frank expression of his views on the future of Indo-China to date:

> I saw Halifax last week and told him quite frankly that it was perfectly true that I had, for over a year, expressed the opinion that Indo-China should not go back to France but that it should be administered by an international trusteeship. France has had the country . . . for nearly one hundred years, and the people are worse off than they were at the beginning.

Roosevelt then added:

> As a matter of interest, I am wholeheartedly supported in this view by Generalissimo Chiang Kai-shek and Marshall Stalin. I see no reason to play in with the British Foreign Office in this matter. The only reason they seem to oppose it is that they fear the effect it would have on their own possessions and those of the Dutch. They have never liked the idea of trusteeship because it is, in some

---

[45] Halifax's own feeling about Roosevelt's verbal statements was that "the President was one of the people who used conversation as others of us use a first draft on paper . . . [that is, as] a method of trying out an idea. If it does not go well, you can modify it or drop it as you will. . . ." Lord Halifax, *Fullness of Days* (London: Collins, 1957) , p. 263.

[46] Hull *op. cit.,* II, 1596.

circumstances, aimed at future independence. This is true in the case of Indo-China.

Each case must, of course, stand on its own feet, but the case of Indo-China is perfectly clear. France has milked it for one hundred years. The people of Indo-China are entitled to something better than that.[47]

By the summer of 1944, however, Roosevelt reluctantly modified his international trusteeship plan. The United States plan for dependent peoples presented at the Dumbarton Oaks Conference in August-September contained no reference to the ultimate independence of European colonies. It stated rather that the trusteeship system of the future United Nations should apply to three categories of territories:

    a. territories then under mandates of the League of Nations,
    b. territories taken from enemy states as a result of the war,
    c. territories *"voluntarily* [my italics] placed under the system by states responsible for their administration."[48]

This trusteeship plan was not discussed at Dumbarton Oaks. Instead "it was left there for further exploration and study by the participating Governments."[49] Yet, points "a" through "c" as above, with only slight changes in style and none in meaning, were approved by the Big Three at Yalta in February 1945, and these principles were finally adopted at the San Francisco Conference in the spring of 1945. Although the plan submitted by the United

---

[47] *Ibid.*, p. 1597. See also "Memorandum by President Roosevelt to the Secretary of State," January 24, 1944, in *Foreign Relations of the United States, Diplomatic Papers 1944, the British Commonwealth and Europe, op. cit.* p. 773.

[48] *Documents of the United Nations Conference on International Organization, Vol. III: Dumbarton Oaks Proposals, Comments, and Proposed Amendments, UN Organization* (London and New York), pp. 607–608.

[49] Testimony by Leo Pasvolsky in *The Charter of the United Nations,* Hearings Before the Committee on Foreign Relations, U.S. Senate, 79th Cong., 1st Sess., (Washington: G.P.O. 1945), p. 226.

States at Dumbarton Oaks did not name Indo-China at either Yalta or San Francisco, it had great policy implications: if Indo-China were to be placed under an international trusteeship, France would have to do this voluntarily, which was highly unlikely.

There were several reasons why the United States Government abandoned Roosevelt's idea of placing colonies such as Indo-China under international trusteeship. One reason was that the Joint Chiefs of Staff felt that the United States should have trusteeships over Japanese islands in the Pacific for military purposes necessary to the national security of the United States. There would thus be a glaring inconsistency in United States policy if she insisted that the European colonial powers place their colonies under international trusteeship.[50] The most important reason, however, was the failure of the United States Government to win support for its plan from Britain and France.

Britain had opposed the international trusteeship plan from the outset. At a press conference given by President Roosevelt on the *U.S.S. Quincy,* when he was returning from Yalta, Roosevelt recalled discussions regarding trusteeship for Indo-China at Cairo and Tehran:

> Stalin liked the idea. China liked the idea. The British didn't like it. It might bust up their empire, because if the Indo-Chinese were to work together and eventually get their independence, the Burmese might do the same thing to England. . . .

And when asked by a reporter whether Churchill wanted

---

[50] According to Hull, "We [the President and the State Department] encountered resistance from our own War and Navy Departments, which felt that our ideas conflicted with their desire to acquire sovereignty of Japanese islands in the Pacific for use as United States bases. We were accordingly not able to bring before the Dumbarton Oaks Conference our dependent peoples project, embraced within a plan for a trusteeship system to be set up under the United Nations organization. Hull, *op. cit.,* II, 1706–1707.

the colonies "all back just the way they were" before the war, Roosevelt answered, "Yes, he is mid-Victorian on all things like that. . . . Dear old Winston will never learn on that point. . . ."[51]

De Gaulle also firmly opposed Roosevelt's trusteeship plan for Indo-China. De Gaulle hoped that he could influence Roosevelt to moderate his stand on independence by announcing publicly his plans to grant Indo-China a greater degree of self-government after the war. De Gaulle first announced a new postwar status for Indo-China in a speech in Algiers on December 8, 1943. According to de Gaulle:

> France intends to give a new political status within the French community to these people who have thus shown their national feeling and sense of political responsibility. The liberties of the various countries belonging to the Union will be extended and reaffirmed within the framework of a federal organization, and the liberal character of their institutions will be emphasized without losing the original imprint of Indo-China's culture and traditions, and finally, the Indo-Chinese will be given access to all public offices and positions in the state. . . .[52]

The next occasion for de Gaulle to stress to the United States Government that he intended to grant Indo-China a larger measure of autonomy came in July 1944 when he visited the United States. The subject of Indo-China was brought up in his meeting with President Roosevelt on July 6. At this time de Gaulle impressed upon Roosevelt his intention to grant Indo-China more representation within a postwar French federal system. On July 10, de Gaulle received a chance to announce publicly his plans for a more liberal policy toward Indo-China. He was asked

---

[51] Rosenman, op. cit., XIII, 563.

[52] "French Committee of National Liberation: Statement on Indo-China, Algiers, December 8, 1943." Cited by Louise Holborn, War and Peace Aims of the United Nations, 2 vols. (Boston: World Peace Foundation, 1948), II, 862–863.

at a press conference: "Do you hope to recover the Empire intact? I am thinking particularly of Indo-China." De Gaulle replied:

> France is certain that she will recover intact everything that belongs to her, but France is certain that after the war and the human experiences which have been undergone, the form of the French world organization and especially for Indo-China will not be the same as before the tragedy we have experienced.[53]

De Gaulle's visit to Washington was of great importance to future Franco-American wartime relations. As Feis points out, the visit "marked a decisive stage in the return admission of France to the company of the West." De Gaulle made a very good impression on United States Government leaders and influenced Roosevelt to consider the Free French Committee of National Liberation as the "dominant" political authority in France until the French people could hold an election.[54] It is possible that this may have caused the United States not to push the idea of making Indo-China a trusteeship at the Dumbarton Oaks Conference.

In any case, what happened in the months just after de Gaulle's visit made it increasingly difficult for President Roosevelt to press for including Indo-China in any international trusteeship scheme. The Allied victory in France and the establishment of de Gaulle as head of the provisional French Government on October 23, 1944 restricted Roosevelt even further. That Roosevelt was influenced by the change of government in France and by de Gaulle's pledges to modify French rule over Indo-China is evidenced by Roosevelt's statement on March 15, 1945. In a

---

[53] Cited by Arthur L. Funk, *Charles de Gaulle, The Crucial Years 1943–1944* (Norman: University of Oklahoma Press, 1959) , p. 269.

[54] Herbert Feis, *Churchill, Roosevelt and Stalin* (Princeton, N.J.: Princeton University Press, 1957) , p. 321.

conversation with Charles Taussig, adviser on Caribbean Affairs, Roosevelt asserted that French Indo-China "should be taken from France and put under a trusteeship." Taussig recorded the rest of the conversation as follows:

> The President hesitated a moment and then said—if we can get the proper pledge from France to assume for herself the obligations of a trustee, then I would agree to France retaining these colonies [New Caledonia included] with the proviso that independence was the ultimate goal. I asked the President if he would settle for self-government. He said no. I asked him if he would settle for dominion status. He said no—it must be independence. He said that is to be the policy and you can quote me in the State Department.[55]

Before the conference at San Francisco, de Gaulle continued to make clear that Indo-China after the war would have a changed status within the new "French community." On March 24, 1945, the Provisional Government of France stressed that Indo-China would soon enjoy "an autonomy proportionate to her progress and attainments."[56] The French propaganda machine also stressed the virtues of the French community as opposed to international trusteeship. Jean de la Roche, an influential spokesman in the United States for the French Ministry of Colonies, wrote that he believed the French formula of association within the French Union which brought France and her colonies closer together had rendered Roosevelt's trusteeship scheme outmoded.

And we can only be happy about it for if in nearly thirty

---

[55] "Memorandum of Conversation by the Adviser on Caribbean Affairs," March 15, 1945, in United States Department of State, *Foreign Relations of the United States, Diplomatic Papers 1945* (Washington: G.P.O., 1967), I, *General: The United Nations,* p. 124.

[56] "The Provisional Government of the French Republic: Statement on Indo-China," March 25, 1945, cited in Holborn, *op. cit.,* pp. 888–890.

years the colonial peoples entrusted to France or England have not evolved sufficiently to merit another formula than that of narrow tutelage—these nations would have failed in their civilizing mission.[57]

At the San Francisco Conference, the French pointed to the Dumbarton Oaks draft which clearly prohibited intervention in domestic affairs of member states.[58] On May 2, 1945, Foreign Minister Georges Bidault made it clear that any decision on trusteeship for Indo-China would be made by France alone. As he remarked in San Francisco:

> On the principle of trusteeship, on the idea of entrusting backward peoples to the guardianship of the United Nations or to one of them, I feel that it can be done subject to consideration of each individual case. Concerning Indo-China, I must state unequivocally that in the plans submitted by the American Government, and which are now under discussion, territories such as Indo-China, which are not mandated and which have not been taken away from the enemy, are excluded from the discussion and will so remain.[59]

The French argument that Indo-China could be placed under national trusteeship only by the consent of France prevailed at San Francisco. The French Provisional Government of de Gaulle, therefore, had joined with the British in a firm stand for retention of France's prewar colonies.

By the time of the conferences at Dumbarton Oaks, Yalta, and San Francisco, the main postwar objective of the United States was the creation of a United Nations group which would keep the peace. Of particular importance was cooperation with Britain and France in Europe.

---

[57] Jean de la Roche and Jean Gottman, *La Federation Francaise-Contacts et Civilizations d'outre-mer* (Montreal: Editions de l'Arbre 1945), p. 25.

[58] *UNCIO, Int. Org. Documents*, Vol. X (London and New York, 1945), Document 230, pp. 641–665; Document 260, p. 433, and Annex D to Document 111 J, p. 622.

[59] Cited in Holborn, *op. cit.*, p. 892.

The United States thus had to soften its approach on the colonialism issue. Hull describes this dilemma as follows:

> We had frequent conversations with these parent countries, but we could not press them too far with regard to the Southwest Pacific in view of the fact that we are seeking the closest possible cooperation with them in Europe. We could not alienate them in the Orient and expect to work with them in Europe.[60]

If the United States could not prevent France from regaining control over Indo-China by having it placed under international trusteeship, perhaps she could achieve this objective by restricting British and French military operations in the area. Countries victorious in war expect to control immediate postwar developments, particularly in regions where they actually fought. Roosevelt thus tried to prevent the British and Free French from playing a significant role in the liberation of Indo-China from the Japanese.

---

[60] Hull, *op. cit.*, II, 1599.

3

THE WARTIME UNITED STATES EFFORT TO RESTRICT BRITISH AND FRENCH MILITARY OPERATIONS IN INDO-CHINA

Throughout the latter stages of the war, President Roosevelt endeavored to prevent Indo-China from reverting to its prewar status in the French Empire. This was an important factor in the American-British controversy regarding theater command jurisdiction over Indo-China. It was also important in the determination of United States policy toward French resistance forces and intelligence operations in Indo-China.

The American-British Controversy of Theater Command Jurisdiction over Indo-China

Britain's principal aim in Southeast Asia was to restore her prewar power along with that of France. The British were in a better position to achieve this aim after the Allied invasion of France and the establishment of a Provisional French Government in the fall of 1944, for they could more easily collaborate with liberated France.

Evidence of British-French cooperation regarding Indo-China was reviewed in a memorandum sent to President Roosevelt by Under Secretary of State Stettinius on November 2, 1944.[1] Stettinius discussed recent developments

[1] "Memorandum by the Under-Secretary of State (Stettinius) to President Roosevelt," November 2, 1944, in *Foreign Relations of the United States, the British Commonwealth and Europe, 1944*, (Washington: G.P.O., 1965), pp. 778–779.

in Indo-China which had been reported by the American Consulate in Colombo. The first point in the memorandum concerned the question of under which command Indo-China fell. This issue of command was far from purely procedural, for political goals in Indo-China could be much more easily achieved by the country in control of military operations.

In 1942, Indo-China had been placed within the China Theater under the command of Generalissimo Chiang Kai-shek and General Albert C. Wedemeyer.[2] But when the British established the Southeast Asia Command (SEAC) in 1943 under Admiral Louis Mountbatten, they had argued that both commands would operate in Indo-China.[3] The British Staff at the headquarters of the SEAC had forwarded a protest to the British Chiefs of Staff in London, complaining that Indo-China had been included in the China Theater under the new United States Army Commanding General in China, and "urging that Indo-China be included in the SEAC Theater."

Subsequently, as Stettinius reported in his memorandum, a "large" French Military Mission of about fifty persons had arrived in Ceylon on October 24 and had "received American approval and [was] now recognized openly and officially." The leader of the Mission, Lieutenant General Blaizot (formerly Chief of Staff in Indo-China) was described as a "colonial" general. Although the United States had advised the SEAC specifically "that only military, and not political, questions might be discussed with the French Mission, political questions [were]

---

[2] Hurley Message to State Department on Southeast Asia, 1945, in *Military Situation in the Far East,* Hearings Before the Committee on Armed Services and the Committee on Foreign Relations, U.S. Senate, 82nd Cong., 1st Sess., Part 4 (Washington: G.P.O., 1951), p. 2890.

[3] Secretary of State for Foreign Affairs, *Documents Relating to British Involvement in the Indo-China Conflict, 1945–1965,* Cmd. 2834 (London: H.M.S.O., 1965), p. 6. Cited hereafter as *British Involvement in the Indo-China Conflict.*

in fact under discussion." By this time, the British Secret Operations Executive (SOE) was "actively engaged in undercover operations in Indochina." The SOE had been ordered by the Foreign Office to concentrate fully on helping the French and "have nothing to do with any Annamite or other native organizations in Indochina." It was further reported that the SOE "desires severely to restrict OSS operations in the SEAC theatre and to give SOE preeminence or, failing that, to establish combined SOE-OSS operations." Thus in the very critical field of intelligence, the British hoped either to preempt or replace the United States and thereby gain a more influential position in Indo-China.

In his memorandum, Stettinius also passed on to Roosevelt a report from the OSS representative in the SEAC, General William Donovan, that drew more sweeping conclusions:

> There can be little doubt that the British and Dutch have arrived at an agreement with regard to the future of Southeast Asia, and now it would appear that the French are being brought into the picture. . . . It would appear that the strategy of the British, Dutch and French is to win back and control Southeast Asia, making the fullest use of possible American resources, but foreclosing the Americans from any voice in policy matters.[4]

It was thus clear by November 1944 that the British were eager to gain control over military and political operations in Indo-China so that they and the French, rather than the Americans, could determine the postwar status of the colony.

President Roosevelt tried to frustrate the British and French moves. In his reply to Stettinius's memorandum, the President directed that the United States should not

---

[4] In effect, therefore, the British military in Southeast Asia still considered Indo-China to be under the operational command of the United States.

approve any French military mission in Indo-China, that American representatives in the Far East should make "no decisions on political questions with the French mission or anyone else," and that they should tell the British, French, and Dutch that "the United States expects to be consulted with regard to any future of Southeast Asia." Roosevelt further stated that the United States had as yet made "no final decisions on the future of Indo-China."[5]

Unfortunately, Roosevelt still had not made up his mind what to do militarily in Indo-China. Moreover, his directives were restrictive and negative, telling United States representatives in Asia what they should not do rather than what they should do to advance American interests. Persons like Ambassador Patrick J. Hurley, whom Roosevelt had sent as Ambassador to China in August 1944, and General Albert C. Wedemeyer, Chief of Staff and military advisor to Generalissimo Chiang Kai-shek, were continuously left in a quandary as to what specific moves to make.

On November 22, 1944, a few weeks after Roosevelt's reply to Stettinius, the British sent the Department of State an *Aide-Mémoire*,[6] which repeated their requests to Washington first made in August 1944. Britain asked the United States to concur in the following proposals:[7]

1. The establishment of a French military mission under SEAC which would "facilitate the work" of the SOE and OSS and which "would serve as the nucleus of the operational headquarters which may be required

---

[5] "Memorandum by President Roosevelt to the Under-Secretary of State (Stettinius)," November 3, 1944, in *Foreign Relations of the United States, The British Commonwealth and Europe, 1944, op. cit.,* p. 780.

[6] The British Embassy to the Department of State, *Aide-Mémoire,* November 22, 1944, *ibid.,* pp. 781–783.

[7] The British had selected three out of five proposals put before them by the French. For the original five proposals, see Memorandum by the Secretary of State to President Roosevelt "French Participation in Liberation of Indochina," October 10, 1944, in *ibid.,* p. 775.

later." The mission's function "would be primarily to deal with matters concerning French Indo-China and it would not participate in questions of general strategy."

2. The establishment in India of a 500 men [French] "Corps Léger d'Intervention" which would "operate exclusively in Indo-China on Japanese lines of communication." This group would perform along the same line as the OSS and SOE.

3. The participation of France "in the planning of political warfare in the Far East," to be arranged between SEAC and the French Military Mission.

According to the British, the United States Chiefs of Staff had agreed with these proposals "from a military point of veiw," with the exception that "French participation in the planning of political warfare should be restricted to the area of the South East Asia Command." The JCS pointed out, however, that "in their view, French Indo-China was part, not of South East Asia Command, but of the China Theatre and was an American sphere of strategic responsibility." The British claimed that the JCS had recognized that an "act of understanding" had been reached between Admiral Mountbatten and General Chiang "by which both Commanders would be free to attack Thailand and French Indo-China and boundaries between the two theatres would be decided at an appropriate time in the light of progress made by the two forces." The British acknowledged, however, that the JCS had never formally confirmed this agreement.

The JCS had stated that no decision on the British requests could be made until President Roosevelt discussed the Indo-China question with Churchill at the forthcoming Quebec Conference. But the question was never raised at Quebec and therefore "no further progress" had been made on the subject which was "becoming increasingly urgent." The *Aide-Mémoire* stressed that it was vital that

Indo-China be under SEAC since it is situated "on the Japanese land and air reinforcement route to Burma and Malaya." The British Government, therefore, asked that the JCS issue a directive confirming the oral understanding between Chiang and Mountbatten and approving the three requests. The United States was assured, however, that this approval

> would in no way prejudice the question of the ultimate settlement of the boundary between the China Theatre and the South East Asia Command, which, by the agreement between Admiral Mountbatten and the Generalissimo, is at present left open, nor the wider question of the participation of regular French armed forces in the Far Eastern War.

The United States replied to the British Government on December 11, 1944. Unfortunately this reply cannot be found in the State Department files.[8] It may be inferred, however, that this reply was inconclusive since on December 27, 1944, Ambassador Winant reported that J. Bennett, head of the Far Eastern Department in the British Foreign Office, had "expressed his concern that the United States apparently [had] not yet determined upon its policy toward Indo-China." Bennett added, however, that Britain and the United States might find themselves in a "very awkward situation" if the French were not allowed to participate in the liberation of Indo-China.[9] Despite the urgency of the British requests, the United States still refused to allow France to participate in the liberation of Indo-China. Nevertheless the British resolutely continued to pursue their goals in Asia.

The United States diplomat who was prehaps the most aware of British motives and activities in Southeast Asia was Ambassador Hurley. Hurley had become increasingly

---

[8] Reported in *ibid.*, p. 783.
[9] "Memorandum by the Secretary of State to President Roosevelt," December 27, 1944, *ibid.*, pp. 783–784.

distressed with what he considered British imperialist policies, and he grew disappointed with what he felt was Washington's naïveté in both understanding and acting upon the problem.

Hurley began to suspect British postwar goals in Asia almost a year before the end of the war. On November 3, 1944, Sir Horace Seymour, British Ambassador to China, told Hurley that a free and unified China would be a mistake since it would be a trouble maker in the Orient. Seymour was worried that the Europeans' rights to extra-territoriality might be eliminated and their colonies in Southeast Asia might be lost. Hurley reminded Seymour that his attitude and that of the British Government conflicted with the principles of the Atlantic Charter, which stipulated that each state "will respect the right of all peoples to choose the form of government under which they will live."[10]

During this period, General Wedemeyer was also becoming disturbed about British policies in Southeast Asia. On November 15, 1944, Wedemeyer reported that the British, French, and Dutch were making an intensive effort to ensure the recovery of their prewar political and economic positions in Asia. He cited as an example of this effort the establishment of a French military mission in India which was preparing to infiltrate into Indo-China. Wedemeyer thus asked Washington for a policy directive.[11]

The next day, President Roosevelt asked Hurley to "inform Wedemeyer that United States policy with regard to French Indochina cannot be formulated until after consultation with the allies at a forthcoming combined staff conference." Hurley was also asked to keep the President "in-

---

[10] Quoted in Don Lohbeck, *Patrick J. Hurley* (Chicago: Regnery, 1956), p. 321.

[11] "Memorandum by the Assistant to the President's Naval Aide (Elsey)," undated, in *Foreign Relations of the United States, Diplomatic Papers 1945, The Conference of Berlin* (Washington: G.O.P., 1960), pp. 915–921.

formed on activities of the British, French, and Dutch missions, in Southeastern Asia."[12]

On November 26, Hurley informed Roosevelt about the newly created "Council of the Three Empires," which special representatives of England, France, and the Netherlands had formed at Kandy, Ceylon, the headquarters of SEAC. According to Hurley, the primary aim of this organization, founded without the knowledge of the United States, was "repossession" of the European empires in Asia and the "re-establishment therein of the imperial governments." Hurley then advised Roosevelt that he should "expect Britain, France and the Netherlands to disregard the Atlantic Charter and all promises made to other nations by which they obtained support in the earlier stages of the war."[13]

Then in a longer report to the President on January 1, 1945, Hurley warned about the "Southeast Asia Confederacy" which was established by the British at Kunming, China. The secret nature of this organization was evident from the fact that no American diplomatic or intelligence agency in Asia knew anything about its operation. Hurley surmised, however, that one of its aims was to use American supplies to oppose American policy in China and Southeast Asia.[14] Hurley's report to President Roosevelt dealt mainly with China. Nevertheless it also had broad implications for development in Southeast Asia. Hurley summarized for the President what he believed to be the four main purposes of British-French-Dutch propaganda in Asia:

---

[12] Roosevelt Message to Hurley on Indo-China, 1944, in *Military Situation in the Far East, op. cit.*, p. 2889. Hurley later remarked sarcastically in these 1951 hearings that Roosevelt's request was "about like sending a telegram to Washington and saying 'Keep me informed on what is transpiring in Tucson, Ariz.'" (p. 2889).

[13] Hurley's message to Roosevelt, November 26, 1944, in the Patrick J. Hurley Collection, located in the University of Oklahoma Bizzell Memorial Library, Norman, Oklahoma.

[14] Lohbeck, *op. cit.*, p. 323.

1. "to condemn America's effort to unite Chinese military forces as interference in Chinese Government;
2. to keep China divided against herself;
3. to use Chinese and American forces and American lend-lease equipment for reconquest of their colonial empires; and
4. to use propaganda to justify imperialism as opposed to democracy."[15]

On March 24, 1945, Hurley told President Roosevelt "that the French, British and Dutch were cooperating to prevent the establishment of a United Nations trusteeship for Indo-China" since this "would be a bad precedent for the other imperialistic areas in Southeast Asia." He stated further that the British, using American lend-lease supplies and if possible American manpower, would try "to occupy Indo-China and reestablish their former imperial control."[16]

American–British differences over Indo-China continued throughout the war, especially concerning theater command. Churchill wired Washington that he realized occasional difficulties had arisen between Wedemeyer and Mountbatten concerning operations in Indo-China, and he suggested that both he and Roosevelt order the Combined Chiefs of Staff to arrange for "full and frank exchange of intention, plans and intelligence between Wedemeyer and Mountbatten as regards all matters of mutual concern."[17]

On March 22, President Roosevelt replied that he realized both Wedemeyer and Mountbatten were conducting air operations and intelligence missions in Indo-China and that this duplication was wasteful and likely to cause

---

[15] Hurley's message to Roosevelt, January 1, 1945, in the Patrick J. Hurley Collection.

[16] Hurley Message to State Department on Southeast Asia, *op. cit.*

[17] Cited in "Memorandum by the Assistant to the President's Naval Aide (Elsey)," *op. cit.*, p. 917.

"dangerous confusion." Roosevelt thus proposed a solution:

> It seems to me the best solution at present is for you and me to agree that all Anglo-American-Chinese military operations in Indo-China, regardless of their nature, be coordinated by General Wedemeyer as Chief of Staff to the Generalissimo. . . . If you agree to this proposal, I suggest that you direct Mountbatten to coordinate his activities in Indo-China with Wedemeyer.[18]

This proposed solution, however, did not clear up the problem since it was obviously not a compromise. On his way back to China from consultations in Washington during March, Wedemeyer stopped at Mountbatten's headquarters to discuss operations in Indo-China. Still fresh in Wedemeyer's mind was a warning he had just received from Roosevelt:

> that he must watch carefully to prevent British and French political activities in the area and that he should give only such support to the British and French as would be required in direct operations against the Japanese.[19]

Unfortunately, the two commanders left the meeting with different understandings. Wedemeyer thought that Mountbatten had agreed not to undertake operations in Indo-China until he had approved of them. Mountbatten believed that the only thing required was an interchange of information. Thus Churchill directed Mountbatten as follows:

> You may conduct from whatsoever base appears most suitable the minimum pre-occupational activities in Indo-China which local emergency and the advance of your forces require. It is essential, however, that you should keep General Wedemeyer . . . continually informed of your operations. . . .[20]

---

18 Cited in *ibid.,* p. 918.
19 Cited in *ibid.,* p. 917.
20 Cited in *ibid.,* p. 918.

That political motives were predominant in the thinking of the British Government was evident when Churchill wrote to Roosevelt on April 11, 1945:

> Now that the Japanese have taken over Indo-China*
> and that substantial resistance is being offered by French
> patriots, it is essential not only that we should support the
> French by all the means in our power, but also that we
> should associate them with our operations into their country. It would look very bad in history if we failed to support isolated French forces in their resistance to the Japanese to the best of our ability, or, if we excluded the
> French from participation in our councils as regards Indo-
> China.[21]

* Churchill is referring to the Japanese coup of March 9, 1945, which removed French administrative control over Indo-China and set up a puppet Vietnamese government. See *infra.,* pp. 81, 95.

On April 12, President Roosevelt died. Thus it was left for President Truman to answer Churchill on April 14. Truman did not want to inflame the issue, but he wanted to make sure that the British knew the American understanding of the Wedemeyer-Mountbatten agreement. The President thus carefully stated:

> General Wedemeyer reports that his conference with Admiral Mountbatten resulted in an agreement that the latter would notify Wedemeyer when he desired to conduct an operation in Indo-China and that the operation would not be conducted until approval was given by the Generalissimo. Wedemeyer's understanding is that the procedure will be for Mountbatten to notify General Carton De Wiart, who would inform Wedemeyer in his capacity as chief of staff to the Generalissimo. If the proposed operation from SEAC could not be integrated with China Theater plans, then Mountbatten agreed he would not undertake it.[22]

---

[21] Cited in *ibid.*
[22] Cited in *ibid.,* p. 919.

In May it became evident that there was an open disagreement between Wedemeyer and Mountbatten, as they
each followed different policies regarding Indo-China
operations. At that time Mountbatten told Wedemeyer
that he intended to fly twenty-six sorties into Indo-China
to support French guerrilla troops. Wedemeyer was con-
fused since he thought the French Government had placed
all French guerrilla troops in Indo-China under the Generalissimo and therefore subject to his rather than Mountbatten's directives. Wedemeyer then asked specifically:
"What arrangements have been made to ensure that the
equipment furnished guerrilla units is employed against
the Japanese?" No answer came from Mountbatten. The
British Commander did send some messages to Wedemeyer, but they contained no information as to the numbers or locations of the guerrilla units which he was going
to supply. Mountbatten then carried out his air sorties
"without waiting for the consent or approval of Wedemeyer or Chiang Kai-shek."[23]

On May 25, Wedemeyer voiced a strong protest to
Mountbatten:

> It had never occurred to me that you would presume that
> you have authority to operate in an area contiguous to
> your own without cognizance and full authority of the
> Commander of that area. . . . Your decision to conduct
> these operations without the Generalissimo's approval is
> a direct violation of the intent of our respective directives.[24]

Wedemeyer then reported to the JCS his conclusions on
the misunderstanding with Mountbatten. He claimed that
he did not have enough information "to coordinate or
evaluate" Mountbatten's operations and that he could
not carry out Roosevelt's "explicit instructions." He then
added that any lend-lease materials which the United States

---

[23] Cited in *ibid.*
[24] Cited in *ibid.*

was making available to the British in support of French operations in Indo-China should be transferred to the China Theater so that the United States Government would at least get "credit for such support" and so that he could carry out his directive "in screening the nature of operations in the area."[25]

Ambassador Hurley on May 28, 1945, sent a long message to President Truman in which he outlined his views on the Wedemeyer-Mountbatten dispute as well as British-French-Dutch collaboration in Southeast Asia. He repeated his warning of March 24 to Roosevelt that the British would try, using American Lend-Lease supplies and if possible American manpower, "to occupy Indo-China and reestablish their former imperial control." Hurley then warned Truman that Mountbatten was already using American lend-lease supplies and other American resources "to invade Indo-China to defeat what we believe to be the American policy and to reestablish French imperialism." Hurley called Truman's attention to the fact that Mountbatten had recently requested Major General Daniel Sultan, United States India-Burma Commander, "for a large increase in lend-lease supplies that will enable him to defeat the Roosevelt policy in Indo-China and reestablish imperialism in that area."

Hurley recommended to Truman that if he was opposed to Britain's political objectives in Indo-China, the United States should stop giving Mountbatten lend-lease supplies and prevent his use of the United States Air Force and other American resources. Hurley reiterated his belief that the British-French-Dutch attempt to use American resources "to enable them to move with force into Indo-China is not for the purpose of participating in the main battle against Japan," but of re-establishing imperialism in Indo-China and placing British forces "in a position where

---

[25] Cited in *ibid.*, pp. 919–920.

they could occupy Hong Kong and prevent the return of Hong Kong to China."[26]

Despite United States awareness of their activities, the British pressed on to increase their political and economic operations in Indo-China. For on May 31, Wedemeyer sent a personal message to General Marshall which, endorsing Hurley's views on British intentions in the Far East, warned once more against increasing British attempts to recover prewar prestige and economic advantage in Southeast Asia. Wedemeyer also suggested that the British would probably propose at the next Big Three Meeting that the boundaries of Mountbatten's command be extended to include all former British, French, and Dutch colonies.[27]

The Wedemeyer-Mountbatten dispute over command of operations in Indo-China was finally resolved in Britain's favor at the Potsdam Conference. Here the Combined Chiefs of Staff allotted to SEAC for occupation the part of Indo-China situated south of 16°N, and north of that line to the Chinese.[28] This was an extremely important decision, for placing the southern part of Indo-China under British occupation was a crucial step in the postwar restoration of French sovereignty in their colony.

Why did the United States agree to this Potsdam decision? According to General Wedemeyer, by the summer of 1945 he had accepted *de facto* the primacy of Mountbatten's command over Indo-China. Although Wedemeyer was urged by Generalissimo Chiang Kai-shek to press Mountbatten on this point, the American General explained that he refused to make an issue of it since he

---

[26] Hurley Message to State Department on Southeast Asia, *op. cit.*

[27] Cited in "Memorandum by the Assistant to the President's Naval Aide (Elsey)," *op. cit.*, pp. 920–921.

[28] "Extract from the Report to the Combined Chiefs of Staff by the Supreme Allied Commander, Southeast Asia, 30 June, 1947," in *British Involvement in the Indo-China Conflict, op. cit.*, pp. 47–52.

knew the war was ending and other matters seemed more important.[29]

Among the factors which took priority over the command dispute was the prospect of rapid postwar demobilization. By the time of Potsdam, the United States was not anxious to assume occupational duties in countries other than Germany and Japan. With the expected public pressure to "bring the boys back home," the United States Government did not feel it should prepare to occupy liberated European colonies as well. Furthermore, Franklin Roosevelt, who had been the driving force against the postwar reassertion of European colonialism, was now no longer on the scene. In addition, President Truman and the State Department were very reluctant to risk straining relations with America's western European allies, especially in the light of increasing tension in American-Soviet relations. The United States felt that a strong postwar France and Britain were in her best interests, and that the loosening of bonds of their empires might seriously weaken their position in Europe.[30] These were some of the reasons why the United States did not remain firm in opposing the French return to Indo-China. The determination of France, especially of de Gaulle, to regain sovereignty over Indo-China was another important reason.

American Opposition to Free French Attempts to Participate in the Liberation of Indo-China

De Gaulle was resolved that he would try to liberate Indo-China as soon as possible. To de Gaulle, "Indo-China

---

[29] Letter from General Albert C. Wedemeyer to author, January 30, 1967.

[30] See John C. Sparrow, *History of Personnel Demobilization in the United States Army* (Washington: Department of the Army, 1951), and Harry S. Truman, *Memoirs*, 2 vols. (New York: Signet, 1965), I, 556–561, 606–607, 454–455; Hull, *op. cit.*, II, 1599, and Chapter V, pp. 125–126.

eemed like a great ship out of control" which he could
not aid until he "had slowly got together the means of
rescue." As he "saw her move away into the mist," he
"swore to [himself] that [he] would one day bring her
in."[31] To accomplish this, de Gaulle realized that French
participation in the actual fighting in Indo-China was a
necessity, for

> it was inconceivable that on the one hand the state and the
> people of the Federation and on the other the Allies would
> countenance the restoration of French power on territories
> where we had taken no part in the world-wide struggle.[32]

Thus if the French "took part in the battle—even though
he latter were near its conclusion—French blood shed on
he soil of Indo-China would constitute an impressive
claim."[33]

De Gaulle also realized that he needed American mili-
ary aid to participate in any liberation venture.. The first
free French request to the United States to participate in
Indo-China military operations had been made in the
all of 1943. On October 20, the Washington Delegation
of the French Committee on National Liberation sent a
memorandum to the State Department, enumerating rea-
ons for French participation in military operations in
Indo-China. The French claimed that they possessed very
useful "documentation and experience," and that they
had important interests in the colony. They also reminded
he United States of "the role which France has traditionally played in the Far East," and warned of "the great
danger" if the Chinese were to liberate Indo-China. The
French argued that such action by the Chinese would
cause "the whole Indo-Chinese population to rise against
he Allies" since the Chinese were the "hereditary enemy"

---

[31] De Gaulle, *op. cit.*, I, 160.
[32] *Ibid.*, II, 625.
[33] *Ibid.*, III, 855.

of the Indo-Chinese. At the very least, though, the French requested that no decision regarding Indo-China be taken without their previous agreement.[34]

Adolf A. Berle, Jr., Assistant Secretary of State, wrote a memorandum the next day in which he related the details of a conversation he had with Henri Hoppenot, the representative of the French National Committee who had handed him the above memo. Berle thanked Hoppenot for his information and told him that the problem raised was "primarily for military consideration." Berle then attached a note, however, which revealed the fundamental problem the United States faced regarding military operations in Indo-China. Berle noted that the liberation of Indo-China was not only a military but a political problem. The United States choice, he explained, was whether "we are reestablishing the western colonial empires or whether we are letting the East liberate itself if it can do so." He suggested that the matter "be discussed on a high level with the President for his decision." His conclusion, however, strikingly unsympathetic to the French, was that "if the Chinese can do anything against the Japanese in French Indo-China to the general advantage of the war, I have difficulty in seeing why we should stop them."[35]

A couple of weeks later, on November 2, 1943, John C. Vincent, the Assistant Chief of the Division of Far Eastern Affairs, wrote a memorandum to Berle commenting on the Assistant Secretary's memorandum of October 21. After agreeing with the opinion expressed in Berle's note, Vincent argued that the French charge that the Chinese

---

[34] "Memorandum, the Washington Delegation of the French Committee of National Liberation to the Department of State," October 20, 1943, in *Foreign Relations of the United States, Diplomatic Papers 1943, China* (Washington: G.P.O., 1957), pp. 882–883.

[35] "Memorandum of Conversation, by the Assistant Secretary of State (Berle)," October 21, 1943, *ibid.*, pp. 883–884.

were the hereditary enemy of the Indo-Chinese was "grossly misleading, if not actually false." He explained that historically the Annamites had sought Chinese help to drive out the French and that "it was China's weakness, not Annamite dislike or fear of China, that permitted the French to remain." Vincent's conclusion was that "it is our belief that the Annamites, by and large, have for the Chinese a feeling of friendliness and cultural affinity." Vincent then dealt with the postwar status of Indo-China:

> The postwar status of French Indo-China is a matter of speculation: return to France; international control and even British control. It is our belief that the Annamites are fundamentally capable of self-government and that it should be the objective of any postwar administration to train Annamites to resume the responsibilities of self-government. This objective might be achieved by a continuation of French administration for a definitely limited period or by international administration. There would seem to be no reasonable basis for British administration. In any event, the Chinese Government should be consulted and its views given full consideration in regard to plans for the future of Indo-China.[36]

The French request that the Chinese should not participate in the liberation of Indo-China finally reached President Roosevelt. On November 8, 1943, Acting Secretary of State Stettinius wrote a memorandum to Roosevelt concluding that the State Department believed that Hoppenot's allegations that the Chinese are the hereditary enemies of the Indo-Chinese are "not in accord with the facts."[37] Roosevelt replied to Stettinius the next day that he agreed with the State Department's conclusion and 'that the French presentation of the case is not sufficiently valid to take any action." He then suggested that the JCS

[36] "Memorandum by the Assistant Chief of the Division of Far Eastern Affairs (Vincent) to the Assistant Secretary of State (Berle)," November 2, 1943, ibid., pp. 885–886.

[37] "Memorandum by the Acting Secretary of State (Stettinius) to President Roosevelt," November 8, 1943, ibid., p. 886.

decide what to do since the decision was "essentially a military problem."[38]

Roosevelt's assertion that the liberation of Indo-China was basically a military problem and that the JCS should decide what to do was not allowed to stand very long. On February 17, 1944, Stettinius sent a memorandum to Roosevelt, forwarding a request by the Civil Affairs Division of the War Department for approval of the use of French troops in the liberation of Indo-China and of French nationals in civilian administration and planning.[39] Roosevelt's reply was forthright and unequivocal. He told Stettinius that "no French troops whatever should be used in operations in Indo-China," and that "the operation should be Anglo-American in character and should be followed by the establishment of an international trusteeship over the French colony."[40]

During the next few months, de Gaulle tried to persuade Roosevelt to help transport a French expeditionary corps to Indo-China. In his meeting with Roosevelt in Washington in July 1944, de Gaulle raised this question for discussion. When Roosevelt tried to explain why the United States Government was hesitant to deploy French troops in Indo-China, de Gaulle asked Roosevelt directly: "Is it because you do not wish us to return to Indo-China?" Roosevelt answered: "No, certainly not! But you must understand the realities of the situation!"[41]

---

[38]"Memorandum by President Roosevelt to the Acting Secretary of State," November 9, 1943, *ibid.*, pp. 886–887.

[39] "Memorandum by the Under-Secretary of State (Stettinius) to President Roosevelt" February 17, 1944, in *Foreign Relations of the United States, The British Commonwealth and Europe, 1944, op. cit.,* p. 774.

[40] Cited in "Letter from James Clement Dunn (Director of the Office of European Affairs) to Director of Civil Affairs Division, War Department (General Hilldring)," in Department of State, *Foreign Relations of the United States, The Near East, South Asia, Africa, The Far East,* (Washington: G.P.O., 1965), p. 1206.

[41] "Report Addressed to General de Gaulle by Admiral Fénard, Chief of the Military and Naval Mission to the United States of

This question was again raised with Roosevelt in October 1944 by Admiral R. Fénard. The President told Fénard:

> I know how anxious you are to see your warships take part in the battle against the Japanese. I understand and I myself would like it very much. The question will be studied. . . .

Roosevelt continued that it was necessary to find a general formula "to solve the problem of the relations between the white and yellow races." He proposed that "this could take the form of a general organization in which each country would continue to occupy themselves with the countries in which they are interested at present."[42] Roosevelt's proposal reflected the modification of his earlier trusteeship plans. It was along the lines of Britain's trusteeship ideas, for it envisioned not international but French postwar supervision of Indo-China.

Roosevelt's proposal to Fénard and his earlier reply to de Gaulle in July 1944 were obviously at variance with his opinions expressed numerous times before, and in the next few months the Free French became convinced that the United States was strongly opposed to their participation in the liberation of Indo-China. On January 10, 1945, the French were rebuffed when the JCS vetoed Admiral Fénard's request to obtain shipping across the Indian Ocean to India of two British-equipped French divisions to be placed under SEAC. Admiral Leahy explained to Fénard that the JCS had studied his request but

> it was the consensus of opinion that transportation to the Pacific of such a force would involve an expenditure of money not justified by any assistance that could be expected

America," October 12, 1944, in Charles de Gaulle, *War Memoirs: Salvation, 1944–1946, Documents* (New York: Simon & Schuster, 1960), p. 41.

[42] *Ibid.,* pp. 39–40.

from the French in the accomplishment of the main Allied war objective, which was the total defeat of Japan.[43]

In March 1945, Harry Callender wrote in the *New York Times* that French officials in Paris were disappointed that Washington had shown no enthusiasm "concerning transportation of a French expeditionary force from North Africa to Indo-China." Moreover, according to Callender, the French were disturbed that the United States considered the war against Japan "an American undertaking."[44]

Two days after Callender's report, de Gaulle was quoted as being chagrined at the United States reluctance to transport a French expeditionary corps to Indo-China which he felt should have been sent long ago. De Gaulle stated:

> Until now it has been our lot in this cruel war to be unable anywhere to return to the fight after initial misfortune save with a broken sword or a borrowed one. . . . Out there, as elsewhere, France does all she can to persuade her Allies to make available to her the arms from their arsenals. In the present situation it is not her fault if the forces she has long prepared to aid Indochina are not yet in line beside those of the Allies.[45]

The Free French thus were extremely annoyed at the United States opposition to sending a French expeditionary corps to Indo-China. President Roosevelt had put forth this position to the Allies at both the Malta and Yalta conferences. At Malta, Roosevelt agreed only to such United States military actions in Indo-China as involved no "alignments with the French."[46] And at Yalta, Roosevelt was even more explicit when he argued that France

---

[43] Leahy, *op. cit.*, p. 286.

[44] Harry Callender, "Ill-Armed French Defend Indo-China," *New York Times*, March 13, 1945, p. 11.

[45] *Ibid.*, March 15, 1945, p. 15.

[46] Hull, *op. cit.*, II, 1475, and *Foreign Relations of the United States. The Conferences at Malta and Yalta, op. cit.*, p. 566.

"had done nothing to improve the natives since she had the colony." He then added that de Gaulle had asked for ships to transport French forces to Indo-China. When Stalin asked where de Gaulle would get the troops, Roosevelt replied that "de Gaulle said he was going to find the troops when the President could find the ships," but Roosevelt had remarked that "up to the present he had been unable to find the ships."[47] Roosevelt's position at these two conferences was thus consistent with his anti-colonial policy adopted earlier in the war. It was also consistent with his refusal to aid French resistance groups in Indo-China.

The issue of American aid to French resistance was of little importance until late 1944, after the Allied invasion of Normandy and the subsequent establishment of a Provisional French Government headed by de Gaulle. Not until this time, when the defeat of the Axis powers seemed imminent, was there any significant French underground movement in Indo-China. Heretofore, most French in Indo-China had collaborated with the Japanese not only to avoid what they felt would be the greater hardships of outright occupation, but also to maintain at least the hope of reasserting French control over the colony after the war. This goal, of course ran counter to President Roosevelt's hopes for Indo-China's postwar status.

On October 13, 1944, Roosevelt received a memorandum from Hull who cited a letter which the State Department had received from General Donovan. The Director of the OSS had written:

The staff of the Theater Commander for the CBI theater has under consideration operation plans involving the furnishing or supplies and equipment to resistance groups. It is contemplated that these operations will be under

[47] Bohlen Minutes of Yalta Conference, Roosevelt-Stalin Meeting, February 8, 1945, *ibid.*, p. 770.

American command although there will be collaboration with the French.[48]

Donovan further explained orally to the State Department that the proposed collaboration in assistance to all resistance groups in Indo-China was to be with the French Military Mission at Chungking. Hull concluded that, subject to Roosevelt's approval, the State Department would tell Donovan that

> it has no objection to furnishing supplies and equipment to resistance groups, both French and native, actually within Indochina, nor to American collaboration with the French Military Mission at Chungking or other French officers or officials in furtherance of the contemplated operations or any other military operations in Indo-china for the defeat of Japan.[49]

On October 16, President Roosevelt made a very curt, negative reply. He directed that the United States "should do nothing in regard to resistance groups or in any other way in relation to Indochina. He then added that the question might be brought to his attention later "when things are a little clearer."[50]

It was not until February 1945 that Roosevelt modified his position and agreed to aid the French underground in Indo-China. But Roosevelt stipulated that such aid should not interfere with planned military operations in the colony; that it should be limited to what was necessary to defeat Japan; and perhaps most important, that it should not be construed as an official United States recognition of French interests in Indo-China.[51]

---

[48] Cited in "Memorandum by the Secretary of State to President Roosevelt," October 13, 1944, in *Foreign Relations of the United States, the British Commonwealth and Europe, 1944, op. cit.*, p. 776.

[49] *Ibid.*, p. 777.

[50] "Memorandum by President Roosevelt to the Secretary of State," October 16, 1944, *ibid.*

[51] "Memorandum, Hull for Wedemeyer, 9 February, 1945, and

Despite this official modification in United States policy toward French resistance fighters, they did not immediately receive aid from Washington. When the Japanese, on February 2, 1945, ordered the French Army in Indo-China to disband and disarm, its leaders balked. Yet for any kind of effective resistance, they desperately needed American military aid and supplies. This was especially true after the Japanese, who had become increasingly alarmed by growing resistance in Indo-China as well as their rapidly deteriorating military position in Southeast Asia, staged a coup in Indo-China on March 9, 1945 which forcefully removed French administrative control over the colony. There was only scattered French resistance to the coup. Although many French fought bravely in areas such as Hanoi and Hue, most of the French Army surrendered in less than one day. Thus French resistance to the coup lasted too short a time to allow the United States to muster up any kind of effective assistance. The situation was different, however, regarding several thousand French soldiers under Generals G. Sabattier and M. Alessandri who were forced to flee through the mountains of Tonking and Laos to refuge in southern China.

General Wedemeyer reported this French plight to Washington, yet Washington, despite pleas from Henri Hoppenot,[52] refused to supply him with additional aid to help the French. This refusal can be attributed, in part, to the logistics problems which plagued the China Theater supply network. Wedemeyer was cut off from the outside world except for a very tenuous line of communications—an air route over the "Hump," i.e., the Himalaya Mountains into the China Theater from India. According to

McFarland for Marshall, 13 March 1945, Msg WX-55402, Wedemeyer to Chennault, 19 March 1945, and other papers in F.I.C., Book I, China Theater Files, cited by Marcel Vigneras, *United States Army in World War II, Special Studies, Rearming the French* (Washington: Department of the Army, 1957), p. 393.

[52] Fall, *op. cit.*, p. 70.

Wedemeyer, this restricted line of communications "greatly limited military operations against the Japanese both on the ground and in the air." Wedemeyer received only a "trickle" of supplies and had to allocate them carefully to the Allied forces under his control, to be used against the Japanese. Since Wedemeyer was preparing for a major offensive against Japan, and since supplies were scarce, any of their diversion to the French in Indo-China might have seemed militarily unprofitable to the JCS, especially since the military situation in Indo-China in effect had become inconsequential in relationship to the grand strategy against Japan. Thus, when the French appealed several times to Wedemeyer for military supplies, he replied that he "did not have sufficient weapons and ammunition available for the Chinese and American forces in the China area." Nevertheless, Wedemeyer did issue blankets and some medical supplies to French forces in Indo-China when he was informed by the French soldiers of the seriousness of their plight and that of their families.[53]

Although logistics and military factors were important, it is more likely that the American refusal to give military assistance to the French resistance fighters in Indo-China was based primarily on political grounds. This conclusion is inferred, for instance, from accounts of French requests

_____

[53] Letter from General Wedemeyer to author, January 19, 1967. See also Wedemeyer's explanation to Sabattier for lack of greater U.S. aid in a letter of April 21, 1945, which stated in part: "Because of the critical shortage of fuel and other supplies in China and also the urgent necessity of providing for our northern front, I very much regret that we are unable to allocate and deliver to you any supplies with the exception of medicines. . . . We will continue, however, to give you tactical air support, attacking as often as possible such objectives as you may designate. For this purpose, we shall maintain one or two air units in your combat area, along with some L-5's to relay your requests and to carry out reconnaissance missions." Quoted in G. Sabattier, *Le Destin de l'Indochine* (Paris: Plon, 1952), p. 206. It must be pointed out that U.S. air assistance to the French in Indo-China did not start until a shift in U.S. policy in late March 1945. See *infra,* p. 84.

for aid from Admiral Leahy and General Claire Chennault, Wedemeyer's Air Commander in Kunming. According to Leahy, Admiral Fénard on March 18 had begged him to release the 14th Air Force supply planes stationed in Yunnan which were loaded with supplies that could have helped the French. But Leahy could not send these planes without Roosevelt's orders, which were not forthcoming.[54]

According to Chennault's account, he was also forbidden to help the French:

> . . . orders arrived from theater headquarters stating that no arms and ammunition would be provided to French troops under any circumstances. I was allowed to proceed with "normal" action against the Japanese in Indochina provided it did not involve supplying French troops. . . . General Wedemeyer's orders not to aid the French came directly from the War Department. *Apparently it was American policy then that French Indochina . . . would not be returned to the French. The American government was interested in seeing the French forcibly ejected from Indochina so the problem of postwar separation from their colony would be easier* [my italics].

Chennault then pointed to the striking difference between the American and British policies:

> While American transports in China avoided Indochina, the British flew aerial supply missions for the French all the way from Calcutta, dropping tommy guns, grenades, and mortars.[55]

A further indication that Roosevelt's determination to prevent the French from regaining control over Indo-China was still United States policy came during Roosevelt's meeting with Wedemeyer in March. According to Wedemeyer, Roosevelt "evinced considerable interest in

---

[54] Leahy, *op. cit.,* p. 338.
[55] Claire L. Chennault, *Way of a Fighter* (New York: Putnam, 1949), p. 342.

French Indo-China and stated that he was going to do everything possible to give the people in that area their independence."[56] Furthermore, Roosevelt told him that after the war he would try to eliminate all colonial systems in the Far East. At the end of the conversation, however, Roosevelt gave him one instruction which he repeated for emphasis, namely, "not to give any assistance whatsoever to the French in Indo-China."[57]

Later, at a lunch with Secretary of War Stimson, when Wedemeyer recounted the instructions Roosevelt had given him concerning the French, Stimson "expressed surprise" and suggested that Wedemeyer mention this to General Marshall.[58]

What seems clear, therefore, as Fall points out, is that Roosevelt's personal instructions to Wedemeyer differed significantly from what had been the agreed upon policy in Washington regarding aid to French resistance in Indo-China.[59] Evidently Roosevelt's strong opposition to the return of French control over Indo-China still held sway. As historians Charles Romanus and Riley Sunderland noted,

> the War Department's response to reports of fighting in Indo-China showed that the United States Government was most reluctant to engage in activity that might result in its being associated with or supporting French colonialism.[60]

The actual change in United States policy toward helping French resistance groups in Indo-China did not come until late March 1945, when Roosevelt finally allowed Leahy to release Chennault's airplanes for support missions

---

[56] General Albert C. Wedemeyer, *Wedemeyer Reports!* (New York: Holt, Reinhart and Winston, 1958), p. 340.

[57] Wedemeyer's letter to author, January 19, 1967.

[58] *Wedemeyer Reports! op. cit.*, p. 343.

[59] Fall, *op. cit.*, p. 57.

[60] Charles F. Romanus and Riley Sunderland, *Time Runs Out in CBI* (Washington: Department of the Army, 1959), pp. 259–260.

in Indo-China.[61] A memorandum dated April 11, 1945—
the day before Roosevelt died—explained the change in policy as follows:

> . . . There has been a modification of the United States
> attitude with regard to aid to French Resistants in Indo-
> China. The present policy is to give the resistant groups
> all help possible without interfering with our own opera-
> tions. This permits liaison between the French in order
> that this aid may be effective. There will be no material
> aid to the French not previously authorized by Headquar-
> ters, China Theater.[62]

The American aid, however, came too late to prevent the
Japanese from killing large numbers of those French soldiers trying to flee to China.[63]

The memorandum of April 11, in addition to outlining
the new American policy toward French resistance groups,
warned that this change "does not permit the United States
Forces to become committed to any political group seeking
to control French Indo-China."[64] This warning was particularly important since it foreshadowed the policy of neutrality in Indo-China's affairs which the United States
officially adopted at the end of the war. The United States,

---

[61] Leahy, *op. cit.*, p. 338. See also Chennault's message to Wedemeyer of March 19, 1945, regarding a report that an "informal
statement of new attitude U. S. government is to help French provided such aid does not interfere with planned operations," and
that "The 14th Air Force may undertake operations, against the
Japanese in Indo-China to assist the French within the limitations
imposed by the above policy." Message, CM-out 55402, Chennault
to Wedemeyer, 19 March 1945, F.I.C., Book I.

[62] "Memorandum, Paul Caraway (Deputy Chief, TPS) to Assistant Chief, G-5," April 11, 1945, in F.I.C., Book I, General Wedemeyer's Files, World War II Reference Branch, National Archives
and Records Service, Alexandria, Virginia.

[63] For a good account of this problem, see Sabattier, *op. cit.*
p. 455.

[64] "Memorandum, Paul Caraway (Deputy Chief, TPS) to Assistant Chief, G-5," April 11. 1945, *op. cit.*

therefore, would no longer actively work against France's attempts to regain control over Indo-China. Indeed, after April 11, the United States would give some assistance. This policy affected all American operations in Indo-China, including the crucial area of intelligence.

UNITED STATES INTELLIGENCE OPERATIONS IN INDO-CHINA AND AMERICAN-FRENCH RELATIONS.—Significant French intelligence activities in Indo-China began in the latter part of 1944. Shortly after the Allied invasion of France and the setting up of a Free French Government in France, the Direction Générale Études et des Recherches (DGER), the Free French intelligence organization, which had been working during the war in Calcutta with the British force 136, Britain's elite commando and intelligence unit, began to make contacts with Frenchmen in Indo-China. An embryonic resistance movement was developed, concentrating within the French Army but also including "politically advanced" Vietnamese. At first, these operations were undertaken even without the knowledge of Admiral Jean Decoux, the French Governor-General.[65]

The American Office of Strategic Services (OSS) had been operating in southern China since 1942. It was not until late in 1944, however, that it began to spread its operations into northern Indo-China. The DGER had worked with the OSS in China, and United States intelligence agencies had maintained liaison officers at theater headquarters.[66] Thus from the start there was fairly close contact between these two clandestine organizations.

Despite close contact with French intelligence in China, the OSS in Indo-China was under orders not to help France politically in her attempts to regain control over her colony. President Roosevelt sought to protect himself from possible domestic political charges that he was aiding French

---

[65] Decoux, op. cit., Part 3, Chap. IX.
[66] Romanus and Sunderland, op. cit., p. 259.

colonialism. Thus in accordance with his change in policy regarding military aid to French resistance groups in Indo-China, he—and Truman after April 12—decided to restrict such aid for intelligence and rescue purposes only. Thus General Wedemeyer, on May 2, 1945, issued the following directive to his commanding Generals in the China Theater:

> U. S. Forces in China Theater will supply arms, ammunition, munitions, and/or other equipment to French forces or the forces of other nationals in FIC [French Indo-China] *only when such is essential in the execution of intelligence . . . and/or rescue projects* approved by the Commanding General, U. S. Forces, China Theater. The equipment furnished to forces in FIC will be limited to that actually required for personal protection of American personnel and/or American units [my italics].[67]

A similar distinction was made by the United States when, on June 6, 1945, China Theater headquarters agreed to joint intelligence activities in Indo-China of the OSS and DGER. The United States insisted that its interest in these joint operations was "purely operational," and in no way was concerned with helping the French regain political control of Indo-China.[68]

From the French point of view, an indication that the United States was still trying to prevent French military operations from leading to French political control of Indo-China came in a conversation between General Wedemeyer and General G. Sabattier on June 4, 1945. According to Sabattier, Wedemeyer told him that military operations in Indo-China would be under the general control of the China Theater, but that French troops to be used against the Japanese were to be under the control of the OSS. This

---

[67] "Memorandum, Wedemeyer to Commanding Generals," May 2, 1945, in General Wedemeyer's Files.

[68] The United States Army, Ms. "History of the China Theater," Chap. 15, p. 13.

shocked Sabattier who claimed that he had understood from a previous conference with Wedemeyer that the United States would furnish radio posts and would parachute equipment to a coordinated troops network under his control. When Sabattier heard what he considered Wedemeyer's new directive, he concluded that the American general was acting under different orders, perhaps as a result of a protest from the OSS.[69]

Wedemeyer asserts that Sabattier accurately reported the essence of this discussion, but that the French general was misinformed on one point and misinterpreted another. Wedemeyer insists that he never agreed to furnish radio or any other type of equipment directly to the French by parachute or by any other means, for he was not authorized to do so by the JCS. Moreover, it seemed to Wedemeyer that OSS control over anti-Japanese operations would probably be the most effective arrangement from a military point of view. Sabattier's suggestion that Wedemeyer was acting under a protest from the OSS was thus a reflection more of the French Commander's frustration than of reality. For as Wedemeyer himself concludes, Sabattier "was understandably quite emotional about the restrictions that I laid down concerning his participation in the operations in his theater."[70]

This episode suggests that Wedemeyer was continuing Roosevelt's policy on French military operations in Indo-China. It also suggests, however, that Sabattier thought Wedemeyer would be much more sympathetic to his requests for aid because of an expected softening in Washington's position after Roosevelt's death.

THE EFFECTS OF ROOSEVELT'S DEATH ON AMERICAN INDO-CHINA POLICY.—After Roosevelt died, Truman swore he would continue Roosevelt's policies if possible. But with-

---

[69] Sabattier, op. cit., pp. 455–462.

[70] Wedemeyer's letter to author, January 30, 1967.

out clear written policies and directives to follow, Truman found it difficult to follow up his predecessor's Indo-China policies. Moreover, it seems that Truman did not look upon the reimposition of French control in Indo-China in the same hostile way as did Roosevelt who made his opposition almost a personal crusade. Philippe Devillers, the noted French scholar on Indo-China, attaches considerable importance to Roosevelt's death as a turning point in United States Indo-China policy. He claimed that with Roosevelt gone, there was a good chance that the United States would reverse its original plans for Indo-China. He asserted that Mountbatten had told de Gaulle, who was visiting Washington after Roosevelt's death, that the French leader had "a good chance of getting satisfaction, for Roosevelt is no longer around. If Roosevelt were still alive, you couldn't return to Indo-China."[71]

De Gaulle himself has acknowledged that Roosevelt's death gave him an opening to return to Indo-China. He noted in his *Memoirs* that in the early summer of 1945

> we witnessed a singular reversal of Washington's attitude toward the value of French military aid. Early in July the Pentagon even asked us if we would be disposed to send two divisions to the Pacific.

De Gaulle then added that as a result of the collapse of the Japanese after the American atomic bomb attack, also collapsing was the "American veto which had kept us out of the Pacific. Indochina from one day to the next became accessible to us once again."[72]

---

[71] Philippe Devillers, *Histoire du Viet-Nam de 1940 à 1952* (Paris: Editions du Seuil, 1952), pp. 149–150. Devillers also alleges that after the Japanese surrender, on the battleship *Missouri*, General Douglas MacArthur told General Philippe Leclerc: "If I could give you some advice, bring troops, more troops, as many as you can" (p. 150). These points were also stressed by Jean Lacouture, French journalist and author, in an interview with this author, on June 6, 1966.

[72] De Gaulle, *op. cit.*, III, 925, 926.

On August 22, 23, and 25, 1945, de Gaulle met with Truman in Washington. He noted that Truman differed from Roosevelt both in his estimation of France's capabilities and intentions in Indo-China and in what operations he would allow the French to perform there. De Gaulle asserted that in his last visit to the United States, France "was still regarded as an enigmatic captive. Now she was considered as a great ally, wounded but victorious, and above all, needed." Furthermore, de Gaulle noted that Truman's words "suggested an attitude remote from the vast idealism which his illustrious predecessor had developed in the same office." According to de Gaulle, Truman concluded that the new threat posed by Soviet Communism was now paramount so that United States dissension with her European allies must be avoided at all costs. Truman's final remark, however, was perhaps the sweetest to de Gaulle's ears. Truman stated that "in any case, my government offers no opposition to the return of the French army and authority in Indochina." De Gaulle then assured Truman, just as he had assured Roosevelt in their meeting in July, 1944, that France would establish a regime "in harmony with the will of the people."[73]

---

[73] *Ibid.*, p. 910. In a press conference held at the French Embassy in Washington on August 24, 1945, de Gaulle discussed his plan for the new status of Indo-China: "The position of France with respect to Indo-China is very simple. France intends to recover her sovereignty over Indo-China. Of course, she also intends to introduce a new regime, but for us sovereignty is a major question. . . . Indo-China must have an Indo-Chinese Government, composed of Indo-Chinese as well as of Frenchmen residing in Indo-China and presided over by the representatives of France. Indo-China must have a Parliament composed of representatives of the various regions of Indo-China. . . . Nevertheless, Indo-China as a whole must have a Parliament which votes on the budget of Indo-China and Indo-China must have its own economic life and must have authority over its own tariffs. In short, there will be an Indo-Chinese Government, and an Indo-Chinese Parliament and an Indo-Chinese economic regime." Cited by Holborn, *op. cit.*, II, 897–898. It should also be noted that one French source maintains that France was sent an American aide-memoire on August 30,

The change in United States policy took some time to filter down to American government personnel in Southeast Asia. The change in Washington, however, was soon striking to Ambassador Hurley. On May 28, 1945, Hurley sent a message to the State Department which shows that the Ambassador was perplexed by what he considered a fundamental change in United States policy. After pointing out that the United States delegation at San Francisco "seemed to support the theory of the imperial control of colonies and dependent nations by the separate or combined imperialistic nations, not by a United Nations trusteeship," he reported "a growing opinion throughout Asia that America favors imperialism rather than democracy." Hurley felt this opinion was unjustified and asked Washington for a policy clarification. He asserted that on May 11 he had asked the State Department whether there had been a policy change at Yalta. The Yalta Conference, it is remembered, had approved the plan for trusteeship put forth by the United States at Dumbarton Oaks. No explicit decision had been made at either conference regarding specific territories, and the agreement at Yalta that, by implication, excluded Indo-China from the trusteeship system had not been made public. On May 18 Hurley was told: "No Yalta decision relating to Indochina known to Department." Hurley also reported in his message that "the French Ambassador and the military mission had become exacting in their demands for American support for the French activities in Indo-China." Furthermore, the French were demanding American war supplies "as a matter of right."[74]

On June 6, Hurley sent another message to the State

1945, which indicated that French sovereignty over all Indo-China "has never been placed in question by The Government of the United States." See R. de L., "L'intervention des troupes chinoises en Indochine à la suite de la capitulation japonais," *Politique Etrangère*, June-July 1950, pp. 22–23.

[74] *Military Situation in the Far East, op. cit.*, p. 2890.

Department wherein he again asked whether there had been any change in U.S. policy toward Indo-China. Hurley pointed out that he had received "definite information" from an unidentified source "that the State Department has advised the War Department of a change in policy in regard to Indo-China." Hurley concluded that "evidence of a change of policy has accumulated to such an extent that we are convinced that there has been a change." In utter exasperation, Hurley maintained that "it would relieve us of considerable embarrassment if the State Department could give us some indication of what the new policy is so that we would not have to continuously state that we have no knowledge of any change of policy and so that we could govern ourselves according to the new policy."[75]

On June 10, 1945, the State Department cabled Hurley that President Truman had wanted him to be fully informed about the current United States Government policy toward Indo-China. Through this cable, Truman informed Hurley that the Yalta decision, which Roosevelt had approved, was that Indo-China would be placed under an international trusteeship only if France consented, and any trusteeship, if accepted, would probably be under French supervision and control. The President did intend, however, "at some appropriate time to ask that the French Government give some positive indication of its intention, in regard to the establishment of basic liberties and an increasing measure of self-government in Indochina before formulating further declarations of policy in this respect."

In the meantime, Hurley was informed, President Truman had explained to the French the current American position on French participation in the liberation of Indo-China and United States aid to French resistance groups in the colony. Truman's explanation to the French had

---

[75] Hurley's message to Acting Secretary of State Grew, June 6, 1945, in the Patrick J. Hurley Collection.

been basically a continuation of Roosevelt's policies. Truman had told them that whereas Americans

> welcome French participation in the war against Japan, the determination of the exact extent that it would be practicable and helpful . . . must be left to the commander in chief of the United States Armed Forces in the Pacific.

Truman wanted Hurley to know that the JCS were then studying the possibilities of French help, according to the following suggestions from the White House:

1. The United States should continue to aid French resistance forces in Indo-China "while avoiding as far as practicable any unnecessary or long-term commitments with regard to the amount or character" of such assistance.
2. United States aid should "not interfere with the requirements of other planned operations."
3. "Large-scale military operations aimed directly at the liberation of Indochina cannot . . . be contemplated at this time."
4. "American troops would not be used in Indo-China except in American military operations against Japan."
5. "French offers of military and naval assistance in the Pacific should be considered on their own military merits as bearing on the objective of defeating Japan. . . ."
6. "There would be no objection to furnishing of assistance to any French military or naval forces so approved, regardless of the theater or operations from which the assistance may be sent, provided such assistance does not involve a diversion of the resources which the Combined Chiefs of Staff consider are needed elsewhere."[76]

What, then, was the change in United States Indo-China

---

[76] *Military Situation in the Far East, op. cit.,* pp. 2892–2893.

policy after Roosevelt's death? On paper, the Truman policy seemed basically a continuation of Roosevelt's, but in actuality there was a subtle change. The key change was the atmosphere in Washington which was ostensibly more cordial and sympathetic to France.

Contributing to this new attitude toward France was the changed war situation. After Germany surrendered on May 8, 1945, the United States Government began to concentrate on the war in the Pacific. The United States sought military support from all its allies to defeat Japan. The Soviet Union had already agreed at Yalta to enter the war against Japan soon after the defeat of Germany. The United States would now also be receptive to France's renewed requests that she be allowed to send troops to Indo-China to help liberate the area from Japan. The French had begun to feel that after Japan was defeated, the United States would be thankful for their aid and sympathetic to their goal of regaining control over Indo-China.

It is this as well as many other problems that made the immediate postwar United States Indo-China policy so difficult. The international trusteeship idea was indeed dead, but there was uncertainty as to what Indo-China policy the United States would now follow.

4

THE POLITICAL SETTING OF AMERICAN POLICY IN NORTH VIETNAM DURING THE IMMEDIATE POSTWAR PERIOD, AUGUST-DECEMBER, 1945

The political situation in North Vietnam at the close of the war was very complex. There were numerous native and foreign groupings, with divergent ideological outlooks and political objectives. The United States was thus faced with a challenging policy problem requiring the utmost political skill and ingenuity.

VIETNAMESE POLITICAL GROUPS.—There were about a dozen native political factions, whose leaders were in varying degrees hostile to one another. All were united, however, in their opposition to the return of French control.

From August 1941 until the Japanese coup on March 9, 1945, the Japanese had controlled Indo-China through the French Governor General of the colony, Jean Decoux. On this day, the Japanese forcefully removed the French government and installed a Vietnamese government which they hoped would be more responsive to their wishes. The head of this puppet government was the Emperor Bao Dai, ruler of the kingdom of Annam, and his prime minister was Tran Trong Kim, a revered scholar. The main political party of this Vietnamese puppet government in Indo-China was the Dai Viet, which tried with only limited success to establish a unified, independent Vietnam. In the fall of 1945, the Dai Viet was unflatteringly described by Arthur Hale. Hale was a representative of the United States Information Agency who based his report of the

95

postwar situation in north Vietnam upon a stay of thirteen
days in Hanoi from October 15 to October 28, 1945, and
upon conversations with American officers who came out
of northern Vietnam later. In November 1945, Hale informed the Department of State that the Dai Viet was a
"rightest mixture of willing and unwilling collaborators
and of 'elite' innocents, all of whom shared strong anti-
French and independence feelings."[1]

By August 18-20, 1945, the government of Tran Trong
Kim, in the wake of the Japanese surrender to the Allies
and the ensuing turmoil in the country, in effect no longer
existed. At this time the Viet Minh, in accordance with
carefully laid plans, took over the reins of government
with only minimal resistance by the Japanese. The origins
of the Viet Minh stem from a decision of the Indo-Chinese
Communist Party (ICP), in accordance with the general
line followed by Communist parties throughout the world
during the war, to form a united front against fascism. On
May 19, 1941, the ICP, together with several non-Communist groups, formed the Vietnam Doc-Lap Dong Minh
Hoi (Revolutionary League for the Independence of Vietnam), popularly known as the Viet Minh. Although the
Viet Minh was a broad front composed of many political
groups and parties and supported by many non-Communist
nationalists, it was controlled by its Communist members.[2]

---

[1] See official report by Arthur Hale to the State Department,
November 1945, p. 1, in the personal files of General Philip E.
Gallagher (The Gallagher Papers), located in the Office of the
Chief of Military History, Washington, D.C. Cited henceforth as
Hale's Report. The intention of Hale in this report was "to con-
centrate on the subjects of public opinion, propaganda, the press
and radio and those factors which would influence any permanent
U. S. information program after a resolution of the present con-
ditions." It is uncertain how this report was used by the Depart-
ment of State, other than as background information.
[2] Buttinger, Joseph, *Vietnam: A Dragon Embattled*, 2 vols. (New
York: Praeger, 1967), I, 344–345; Fall, *Ho Chi Minh on Revolution*.
(New York: Praeger, 1967), pp. 61–62; and Ellen Hammer, *The*

The Viet Minh had been allowed by the Chinese nationalists to organize in southern China in the spring of 1941, when Indo-China had already become a Japanese base. Chiang Kai-shek allowed the founding of the Viet Minh in China because he feared the prospect of Japan's gaining control of the Vietnamese nationalist movement. Moreover, he was incensed at the French for their prewar economic imperialism in China and their concessions during the war to the Japanese in Indo-China.

The leader of the Viet Minh was Ho Chi Minh, who was both a dedicated Communist and a dedicated nationalist.[3] The Chinese Nationalists began to distrust the Viet Minh shortly after its inception since they believed it was directed by Communists. As a result, they imprisoned Ho and established what they hoped would be a more docile nationalist coalition called the Vietnam Cach Menh Dong Minh Hoi (Vietnam Revolutionary League), popularly known as the Dong Minh Hoi. As head of this group, the Chinese placed Nguyen Hai Than, an old Vietnamese nationalist who had worked closely with the Kuomintang in China since before World War I. The Allies hoped that the Dong Minh Hoi would perform valuable intelligence functions in Vietnam, but it soon became clear that only the Viet Minh, which used an elaborate network of party cells throughout Vietnam established previously by the ICP, could provide the desired information. It was for this reason that Chiang Kai-shek, on September 16, 1943, released Ho from prison and appointed him head of the Dong Minh Hoi. In late 1943 and early 1944 both the Dong Minh Hoi and the Viet Minh operated uneasily together in China. It was the Viet Minh, however, still

Struggle For Indochina, 1940–1955 (Stanford: Stanford University Press, 1966), p. 97.

[3] For the best accounts of Ho's background, see Fall, op. cit., pp. 81–103, and Jean Lacouture, Ho Chi Minh (New York: Random House, 1968). For an assessment of Ho by the United States Government in the fall of 1945, see pp. 116–124.

led by Ho, which became the most effective and dominant group upon which the Allies began to rely for intelligence for the rest of the war.

The Viet Minh, moreover, had organized groups of dedicated guerrillas who strove to expel the Japanese from Vietnam. At the close of the war in August 1945, the Viet Minh, led by Ho, began a series of moves directed toward winning independence for Vietnam. On August 16, the Viet Minh announced the creation of the National Liberation Committee of Vietnam. Then by a coup d'etat during August 18-20, the Viet Minh took power and set up in Hanoi a Provisional Government of the Democratic Republic of Vietnam.

In an abdication ceremony at the Imperial Palace in Hué on August 26, Bao Dai called upon:

> all parties and groups, all classes as well as the Royal Family to strengthen and support unreservedly the Democratic Republic of Viet Nam in order to consolidate our national independence. As for us, We have known great bitterness during the twenty years of our rule. Henceforth, We are happy to assume the status of free citizen in an independent country. We shall allow no one to abuse our name or that of the Royal Family to sow discord among Our compatriots. Long live the independence of Vietnam! Long live Our Democratic Republic![4]

After the Viet Minh seized control of the government, it became the dominant Vietnamese political group in north Vietnam. It immediately sought a united front against the French. The Viet Minh program included a promise of general elections to be held on December 23, 1945, and the drafting of a constitution to be submitted to a referendum. The program was sufficiently broad to include all, as Hale put it, except "the most radical and most irreconcilable elements,"[5] such as the Cao Dai.

[4] Cited by Hammer, *op. cit.,* p. 104.
[5] Hale's Report, *op. cit.,* p. 11.

The Cao Dai was a religious group which combined the major religious beliefs of the Vietnamese people—Buddhism, Taoism, Confucianism, and Christianity—into a single religion. Politically, the Cao Dai was anathema to the Viet Minh not only because of the former's strong religious base, but also because it had collaborated with the Japanese during the war. The Cao Dai, on the other hand, detested the Viet Minh (the Communists in particular) who were trying to suppress them. Hale reported that the Cao Dai was responsible for inciting the Annamese masses to mob actions. In his view, such actions were "incompatible with the position of the Provisional Government." In his report, Hale argued that the Ho Chi Minh regime "wanted above all to preserve its face to the western world and to prove itself mature and capable of self-government."[6] Hale insisted that reports issued by Reuters and "enlarged upon" by the French-influenced All India Radio and Chungking Radio were detrimental to the image the Viet Minh was trying to present to the outside world. These reports did not distinguish between acts of the Cao Dai and the Viet Minh, but rather ascribed them all to the Provisional Government.[7]

Besides the Cao Dai, there were other native groups which differed with the Viet Minh, as well as with one another. There were religious sects, such as the Binh Xuyen and Hoa Hao, but far more important were the political groupings. There were at least nine different political groups, the most important being the old Nationalist Party of Tongking (modeled after the Chinese Kuomintang Party), the Viet Nam Phuc Quoc (basically pro-Japanese), and the Dai Viet.[8]

---

[6] *Ibid.,* p. 9.

[7] *Ibid.,* p. 11.

[8] Buttinger states that no historian on contemporary Vietnam has considered it important to list any of the other political groups, and that no political group other than the Viet Minh was of great significance (*op. cit.,* I, 262).

An indication of the differences among these groups was the sprouting of native newspapers covering almost every shade of the political spectrum. There were about seven principal dailies. At times, new partisan publications appeared, but these were usually temporary and tended to disappear almost as suddenly as they were published. There were ten permanent weeklies, although in any given week as many as fifteen might appear on the streets. The large number of papers was an indication not only of the intense political interest of the people but also of the liberal attitude of the Provisional Government. The Viet Minh generally took little notice of "fly-by-night" papers, since they rarely were strongly opposed to its basic policies.[9]

The Viet Minh-led Provisional Government, however, was in complete control of the Hanoi Radio upon which it built its information and propaganda programs.[10] It

---

[9] The seven major papers were *Cuu Quoc* (official organ of the Provisional Government and Viet Minh Party), *Dan Quoc, Vietnam Thoi-Bao* (evening, unofficial government organ) *Co Giai Phong* (organ of the Communist Party), *Quoc-Gia, Thanhnien,* and *Dan Thanh.* These were all one sheet papers, with five or six type columns. There were no accurate circulation figures available. A Government spokesman, according to Hale, claimed that *Cuu Quoc* had a circulation of 75,000 and estimated that *Co Giai Phong* had 25,000 readers. Although Hale felt that these figures seemed "improbable," he did observe that readership in Hanoi was high. Hale "saw Annamites apparently of small means buying two and even three newspapers at the same time. In the busy parts of the city newsboys sold out their bundles almost immediately. When tension was high, as it was on October 23. . . . [Hale] had difficulty finding copies of newspapers in the streets. Press and radio seemed to arouse interest in each other, as Annamites crowded around the loud-speakers at neighborhood propaganda shops to hear the newscasts and commentaries, then hurried to the corner to find a newsboy." Hale's Report, *op. cit.,* p. 4.

[10] Hale reported that in the major cities of Hanoi and Haiphong, the percentage of the population which had radios was "quite high," although no official estimate of the number was available. In the smaller towns and villages, Hale concluded that the percentage was lower, yet it was his "opinion" that the Vietnamese

also controlled most of the propaganda shops in Hanoi. These Government operated news and information centers, according to United States observations, were "virtually pivots of communal feeling and activity." Highlighted were many pictures of local events, demonstrations, meetings, etc., whose captions were mostly "slanted toward unity, freedom, and cooperation."[11] Thus with the main propaganda organs under its control, by September 20 the Viet Minh seemed to be "definitely in the saddle."[12]

After the Viet Minh seized power by the August coup it was faced with the very formidable task of forging Annamese unity out of diversity and of building a viable state socially, economically, and politically. Its task was made much more difficult, however, by British and French charges that it was more a creation of the Japanese than a genuine native nationalist organization.

Harold Isaacs, an American war correspondent in Vietnam who was very sympathetic to the Vietnamese cause, observed at the close of the war that the British and French made several allegations concerning Japanese aid to the Viet Minh and the Provisional Government: first, that the Viet Minh was created by the Japanese and put into power by them; second, that Japanese soldiers deserted to the Viet Minh and became the backbone of Vietnamese resistance against the French; and third, that the Japanese supplied arms to the Vietnamese to fight the French.[13] These charges were reflected, for instance, in the follow-

---

owned about 25 per cent more radio sets than people in comparable areas in China, because of French imports before the war. Hale added, however, that Radio Hanoi had an audience "far greater than the number of receivers would indicate." *Ibid.*, p. 5.

[11] *Ibid.*, p. 6.

[12] See letter from General Gallagher to General R. B. McClure, Chinese Combat Command, USF, CT, APO 286, 20 September 1945, in the Gallagher Papers.

[13] Harold R. Isaacs, *No Peace for Asia* (New York: Macmillan, 1947), pp. 154–164.

ing remark made by the British Foreign Secretary in the House of Commons on October 24, 1945:

> In Indo-China as in Java the Japanese followed a policy of encouraging the growth of nationalism and with Japanese backing and arms nationalist groups were able in August last to establish what has become known as the Viet-Nam Republic. . . .[14]

But how accurate were these charges? That the Viet Minh was a creation of the Japanese seems to have been a fiction created by news media rather than a reality. News reports from Vietnam, which were issued almost exclusively by Reuters and by the All India Radio and Chungking Radio, either stated or implied that Ho's Provisional Government had been a creation of the Japanese forces. Moreover, statements by British and French officials were designed to foster this impression, particularly in the United States, in order to gain American support for the reimposition of French and British control over their Southeast Asian colonies. French High Commissioner D'Argenlieu, for instance, said on November 25, 1945 that "conversations with the Annamites to settle differences are progressing favorably and we have promised not to prosecute Annamite leaders as war criminals."[15]

This charge overlooks the fact that the Viet Minh drew its greatest strength from indigenous roots. Thus as Buttinger explains, support of the Viet Minh became "identical with the national resolve to defend the country's new-won freedom. . . . One might look at the Vietminh Government [in August 1945] as one might a train going where the entire nation wanted to go, the only train people could board. . . ."[16] This charge also ignores the fact that the Viet Minh from its inception had fought the Japanese.

---

[14] Doc. No. 4, *British Involvement in the Indo-China Conflict.*
[15] Quoted in Hale's Report, *op. cit.,* p. 12.
[16] Buttinger, *op. cit.,* I, 345.

According to Hale's report, it was the Viet Minh guerrillas who during the war formed the "only genuine activity against the Japanese. . . ." American observers on the scene in September 1945 found that it was "ironical" that the French propaganda barrage after the war stressed Viet Minh collaboration with the Japanese, whereas "relative to their total population in Indo-China the number of Frenchmen active in any resistance movements was pathetically small." These observers also pointed out that those Frenchmen who did resist the Japanese had "nothing but praise for the anti-Japanese work of the Viet Minh and its followers."[17]

It is true, however, that the Japanese in Vietnam, just as in Burma, rallied the native population to their side by their support of independence movements and by such slogans as "Asia for the Asians." Moreover, respect for Japan amongst the Vietnamese increased as a result of her relatively easy takeover from the French in March 1945. The puppet Annamese Government that the Japanese then set up was definitely controlled by Japan. But the Provisional Government set up afterward by the Viet Minh was definitely anti-Japanese. Yet despite continuing anti-Japanese actions by the Viet Minh after the war, such as sharp attacks on the Japanese in the Viet Minh radio and press, it has been asserted that to the Japanese "even a Vietnamese government led by Communists who had been generally anti-Japanese seemed . . . preferable to returning the country to the French." Thus the Viet Minh Government was helped by the "benevolent neutrality of the Japanese."[18] It is also argued that the Japanese High Command after the war actively worked toward supporting those elements whom it hoped would fulfill Japan's historic task of ridding Asia of the white man's imperialism. "Thus, on August 25, 1945, ten days after the Japanese

---

[17] Hale's Report, *op. cit.*
[18] Hammer, *op. cit.*, p. 101.

capitulation, the Vietminh dominated the entire country. It had gained power with disconcerting ease by a combination of negotiations, infiltration, propaganda, and intimidation, but above all thanks to Japanese 'neutrality'. . . ."[19]

Regarding the second accusation, that Japanese soldiers who deserted to the Viet Minh led Vietnamese resistance against the French, evidence is lacking on the exact extent of Japanese desertion to the Viet Minh. There were numerous Japanese desertions, but how many went over to the Viet Minh cannot be determined. The official United States estimate is inconclusive, pointing out that it was "probably true . . . that some [Japanese] put on native clothing and joined the Annamite soldiery."[20] Added information, however, is given by Harold Isaacs, who reported that a United States intelligence team in Saigon arrived at the top estimate of two thousand Japanese deserters out of seventy thousand troops, of whom very few joined the Viet Minh.[21]

Much more evidence is available regarding the third accusation. Isaacs claims that he was told by Viet Minh spokesmen that they received "only a dribble" of arms from the Japanese.[22] Hale's report, however, reveals that the Viet Minh ultimately gained possession of larger quantities of arms from the Japanese. Information obtained by the United States from an interrogation of Lieutenant General Tsuchihashi, Japanese Commanding General, French Indo-China, from talks with Ho Chi Minh, and from inquiries among Frenchmen and Annamese in various positions, reveals the following developments. When the puppet Annamese Government was set up in March 1945, it began to be harrassed by Viet Minh guerrillas. During April,

---

[19] Philippe Devillers, *Histoire du Vietnam de 1940 à 1952*. (Paris: Editions du Seuil, 1952), p. 142.

[20] Hale's Report, *op. cit.*, p. 13.

[21] Isaacs, *op. cit.*, p. 156.

[22] It is unclear whether this reference was to all of Vietnam or just to the southern part where Isaacs was then situated. *Ibid.*

this puppet Government asked Japan for arms to defend itself from what it called "bandit" attacks by guerrillas. At this point, "small quantites of rifles and ammunition were issued" by the Japanese. In the next few months, the puppet Government and the Japanese were both unsuccessful in stopping this Viet Minh harrassment. Therefore in early July, when the puppet Annamese Prime Minister asked Japanese officials in Hanoi for large shipments of arms, "commencing July 20, regular shipments were made." Thus when the Viet Minh guerrillas seized control in August, they captured large caches of arms and ammunition.[23]

When Chinese occupation began in the north in September 1945, there is evidence that the Japanese turned over many weapons and much ammunition to the Viet Minh. According to occupation regulations, these weapons should have been handed over to the Chinese. When this was not done, the highest ranking American official in Vietnam, Brigadier General Philip E. Gallagher, head of the United States Military Advisory and Assistance Group which arrived in Hanoi at about the same time as the Chinese occupation forces, was so disturbed that he made the following report to his Commanding General in China, Robert McClure:

> . . . I am quite positive this turning over of weapons was a deliberate act on the part of the Japs to put into the hands of Annamites the necessary firearms to cause violence against the French, and to complicate Lu Han's* problem. I recommend this Jap general and his division commander and such other senior officers as I may designate at another date be airlifted from here to another area at the earliest possible date . . . They are a source of trouble, and will continue

* Lu Han was the Chinese Commanding General of the occupation forces.

---

[23] Hale's Report, *op. cit.,* pp. 12–13.

to be until they are moved out. Subordinate commanders can be used to take care of the Jap garrisons.[24]

Some Japanese leaders did abide by the occupation regulations and turned over their arms to the Chinese occupation forces. Yet the Chinese sold the Viet Minh many of these weapons, as well as some American weapons given them under the war-time Lend Lease agreement. According to Bernard Fall, the Viet Minh acquired "a total of close to 40,000 weapons, including mortars, artillery, and eighteen tanks."[25] There is thus no doubt that the Viet Minh did receive considerable amounts of weapons both directly and indirectly from the Japanese. There is no evidence, however, that these arms received after V-J Day formed the main source of supply to the Viet Minh. The Viet Minh did steal large stacks of French arms which were poorly guarded by the Japanese. But perhaps a larger portion of the arms in the hands of the Viet Minh had been received from United States agencies.[26]

In reviewing the three accusations of Japanese aid to the Viet Minh, it may be concluded that there were elements of truth in each. The important point, however, is that these accusations seem to have been incorrect in their emphasis. Contrary to the implications of these allegations, the Viet Minh Government was not installed by the Japanese, Japanese deserters did not form the backbone of the Viet Minh forces, and Japanese arms did not provide the main firepower for the Viet Minh resistance against the French.

THE CHINESE OCCUPATION FORCES—In order to understand the actions of the Chinese forces during the occupation

---

[24] Letter from Gallagher to McClure, *op. cit.*

[25] Bernard Fall (ed.), *Ho Chi Minh on Revolution* (New York: Praeger, 1967), p. 146n.

[26] See Chap. V, pp. 118–119.

period, it is necessary to review China's interest in Vietnam during the war.

During the war, the Chinese Nationalists seemed to be acutely aware of the strategic importance of the Indo-Chinese peninsula and of the opportunity to eliminate French imperialism in China. China was interested especially in ending French concessions and special privileges in China and removing French control of the Hanoi-Canton railroad. This awareness was underscored, for instance, in statements by Dr. Chu-Koching, President of Chekiang University. In a Chinese newspaper in the summer of 1942, Dr. Chu stressed the importance of Indo-China as an outlet to the sea for southwest China, and as an outpost for defense. And at a conference shortly thereafter, Dr. Chu concluded that China could not allow Indo-China, whose surrender in 1940 had given Japan significant strategic advantages in Asia, to return to French control after the war. Instead he advised China to ask for the independence of Indo-China and even to offer to become its tutor.[27]

In keeping with their anti-French attitude, the Chinese Nationalists organized Vietnamese revolutionaries into the Dong Minh Hoi. They also erected along the Chinese-Vietnamese border a widespread espionage network which was designed to prevent communication between the French military missions in China and French resistance elements in Vietnam.[28] They refused, however, an offer by President Roosevelt to take over Indo-China completely after the war.[29]

When Chinese occupation forces entered northern Viet-

---

[27] OSS, R&A Report No. 26171, Amemb Chungking, August 18, 1942, cited by Bert Cooper *et al., Case Studies in Insurgency and Revolutionary Warfare: Vietnam, 1941–1954* (Washington: Special Operations Research Office, the American University, 1964), p. 106.
[28] OSS-R&A Report No. 62170, US Congen Kunming. Des No. 2063, January 24, 1944, cited by *ibid.*
[29] See Chap. II, pp. 47–48.

nam on August 28, 1945, they were confronted by ambiva-
lent feelings on the part of the Vietnamese. The Vietnamese were aware that the Chinese during the war had
pushed for Vietnam's independence from France, yet they
were afraid that the Chinese might try to impose their own
control. So strong was this anti-Chinese feeling that Vietnamese forces fired upon the first Chinese troops which
crossed into Vietnam.[30] Moreover, when Chinese soldiers
arrived in Hanoi on September 9, Vietnamese fought them
in the streets.[31] Vietnamese anger was directed especially
against those Chinese soldiers who stole rice and other
food, for Hanoi was afflicted then with a serious food
shortage.[32] Thus when the Chinese occupation forces
spread through the country, they revived Vietnam's traditional fear of Chinese power and territorial ambition.

Also important was the Vietnamese hatred of Chinese
economic imperialism. The Chinese throughout Southeast
Asia had traditionally been among the shrewdest and most
successful businessmen. They often were despised by the
natives who usually were not so successful. This disparity
in business success and wealth was often attributed to the
fact that the Chinese were "outsiders" who employed without compunction all sorts of chicanery and insidious economic devices to cheat the natives. In northern Vietnam
after the war, this anti-Chinese feeling was widespread.
It quickly intensified, moreover, as a result of the "undis-
ciplined excesses" of the Chinese Nationalist soldiers. As
one Japanese military officer observed:

The hostile resentment of the Annamese, first pointed
toward the French, was gradually shifted toward the Chi-

----

[30] Hale's Report, *op. cit.*, p. 16.

[31] *New York Times,* September 19, 1945.

[32] Interview with Vietnamese graduate student in Boston who
wishes to remain anonymous, February 23, 1968. This student was
a youth in Hanoi during the period 1944–1954. He adds that these
riots were of "minor significance."

nese Nationalists. So were the rifles of the Annamese independence forces. In all parts of the city [Vinh], clashes arose
between Chinese Nationalist troops and units of the Annamese Independence Army. Unable to bear the atrocities of
the Chinese Nationalist soldiery, the Annamese population
of Vinh had decided to launch a city-wide strike. . . .

The strike was unsuccessful because of the harsh repression
of the Chinese soldiers.[33]

This anti-Chinese feeling among the Vietnamese was
inflamed by French propaganda disseminated by the
French mission under Major Jean Sainteny. Serious outbreaks of anti-Chinese violence were avoided only by the
continual reassurance of the people by Ho's Provisional
Government, through the press and radio of the good
faith of the Chinese.[34] Furthermore, General Lu Han did
all he could to ease Vietnamese apprehension by repeatedly
stating that the Chinese were in Vietnam only as occupation
forces to supervise the Japanese surrender and to maintain
"law and order." He repeatedly asserted that China had
no territorial designs on Vietnam whatsoever, and he
stressed that the Chinese would remain neutral between
the Vietnamese and French. When the occupation nature
of the Chinese mission was finally made clear by the combined efforts of the Provisional Government and Lu Han,
the Vietnamese nevertheless, according to some American
observers, "accepted the situation with resignation rather
than enthusiasm."[35]

As time went on, however, both the masses and the
Provisional Government began to resent the Chinese, particularly because the Chinese soldiers "exercised restraint"
upon them "without a clear indication of political position
or military intention." The Vietnamese, for instance, were

---

[33] Masanobu Tsuji, *Underground Escape* (Tokyo: Booth and
Fukuda, 1952), pp. 113–114.
[34] Hale's Report, *op. cit.*
[35] *Ibid.*

disturbed by the tight censorship imposed by the Chinese in October over all material in the Annamite press and radio which discussed the French and British. Thus, when the Chinese forces began to prepare to withdraw, due to Chiang Kai-shek's pressing problems at home with the Communists, "the Annamites were greatly relieved."[36] China's discussions with the French concerning withdrawal of her occupation troops began in early October 1945 and finally ended on February 28, 1946 with China agreeing to pull out completely by March 31, 1946.[37]

THE FRENCH.—At the close of the war, there were about thirteen thousand French in northern Vietnam. They were a motley group, divided into two principal categories. First, there were discredited Vichy Government officials tainted by accusations of weakness, collaboration, and treason. Detested by the Annamese, they were chiefly interested in Allied protection until they could return to France. Second, there were French Foreign Legion and colonial troops which had resisted the Japanese in the latter part of the war. Most of these men had been incarcerated by the Japanese. There were about 4,500 French who had been held as prisoners of war by the Japanese. Many of these were married and had their families with them in Hanoi. Most of these prisoners had been quartered in the "Citadel" since the coup of March 1945. In general, their living conditions were deplorable, with severe overcrowding, insufficient food, and widespread disease.[38]

These two groups, divided in their backgrounds and outlooks, were none the less united in their support for the return of French rule in Vietnam. Many of the more

---

[36] *Ibid.*

[37] In payment for withdrawal of its troops, China won the French surrender of extraterritoriality privileges in China and railroad rights in Yunnan, and gained free railroad passage for Chinese goods to Haiphong.

[38] See Gallagher letter to McClure, *op. cit.*

enlightened Frenchmen felt that the old type of colonial exploitation was passé and that the Vietnamese should receive at least partial self-government and freedom. This view, however, which was held most strongly by the Gaullists, was unfortunately a minority one. Most French did not have this relatively progressive outlook, owing at least in part to a forlorn hope of returning to the "good old days" of special privileges and soft living.

Most of the French began to resent bitterly the Vietnamese who had assumed control of all the public buildings, utilities, etc. The French were "inwardly chagrined" that the Vietnamese could by themselves run their city administration in a creditable fashion. The French also felt hurt that the Vietnamese did not consider it a blessing to have experienced the benefits of *la mission civilisatrice.* After all, the natives should have been grateful to the French not only for physical improvements of their country, but also for their exposure to French culture. This French feeling was reflected in the following exchange between Harold Isaacs and a French woman in Saigon in the fall of 1945.

"The Annamites astound me," exclaimed the woman. "What more could we have ever done for them than we did? Why, do you know we organized a municipal council here in which they were to have half the seats! Imagine, half the seats! What more could they want?" When Isaacs replied, "All the seats," the woman looked at him "aghast."[39]

The Provisional Government's success at running the country in the north thus shocked the French who felt that the Vietnamese were "too underdeveloped for self-government and that self-rule would result in internecine warfare [among the Vietnamese] and tyrannical dictatorships." There was therefore a wide gap, according to Hale,

---

[39] Isaacs, *op. cit.,* p. 141.

between the expectations of the French and the realities of the situation.[40]

A similar gap was seen by Hale in the French expectation of racial discrimination by the Vietnamese. The French, who seemed "very conscious of color differences," continually spoke of "Asiatic conspiracies against the Caucasian race, of future color wars, of the need to draw together to defend the position of the Westerner in Asia." The French could not forget the anti-white and anti-Western propaganda of the Japanese during the war, and they felt that the yellow Vietnamese shared these feelings with their Japanese racial brethren. But the Vietnamese, according to Hale's report, while afflicted by some anti-white bias, were not so racist as French propaganda would make one believe. Anti-white attitudes, therefore, seemed a product more of French fears and imagination than of reality.[41]

The Vietnamese had other reasons for hating the French. Most Vietnamese felt the resentment against colonial exploitation that is normal among a subject people robbed of their dignity and freedom. Moreover, the Vietnamese were disgusted and bitter at those Frenchmen who had failed to protect Vietnam from the Japanese and even collaborated with the invaders. Their hatred of the French had reached its peak after the March 1945 coup when the French offered virtually no resistance to the Japanese takeover. Thus the Vietnamese, the Viet Minh in particular, despised the French for "selling out" Vietnam to the enemy. As the Viet Minh press and radio charged after V-J Day, "And now you want back the position you wouldn't defend, the unfair oppression of the Vietnamese who alone fought the enemy with whom you collaborated."[42]

This intense hatred was striking to Harold Isaacs who summed up his impressions as follows:

---

[40] Hale's Report, op. cit., p. 18.
[41] Ibid.
[42] Cited by ibid., p. 13.

This hatred of the Annamites for the French was a living, leaping thing in the land. You read it in the faces of the ordinary people, in the faces I saw in the yard of the Saigon Sureté. You heard it in the voices of the educated Annamites, speaking impeccable French . . . It was like a social disease of the subjected, this passionate loathing. Whole generations had been infected with it, by the vermin in French prisons or by the slower poison of an enforced inferiority haunting every step of their lives from cradle to grave.[43]

THE AMERICANS.—As much as the Vietnamese distrusted and hated the French after the war, they seemed to like and even revere the Americans, hoping that they would help Vietnam gain independence. Just as the French were thankful to the British for helping them regain control in southern Vietnam, they looked to the Americans to perform a similar function in the North. Even the Chinese who were in charge of occupation counted upon the Americans for satisfactory execution of their duties.

Thus it was to the Americans that everyone in north Vietnam, both natives and foreigners, looked for help. The Americans could not possibly have satisfied these conflicting aspirations and requests in a manner that would have pleased all. What policy then did the United States Government decide upon to resolve this dilemma?

---

[43] Isaacs, *op. cit.*, p. 146.

5

UNITED STATES POLICY TOWARD VIETNAM IN THE IMMEDIATE POSTWAR PERIOD

At the end of World War II, the United States was confronted with many serious diplomatic problems. Vietnam, however, was not considered by Washington to be among the most important. Neither General Wedemeyer nor the groups of Americans in Vietnam, therefore, received the attention and direction from the State Department which might have resulted in a clearer expression and execution of policy.

Throughout the war and the immediate postwar period, the United States stressed a "Europe-first" policy. This was determined largely by America's military decision that Europe was the decisive theater of world conflict.[1] It was also consonant with the American tradition of "Europocentrism" which had roots in the national origin, cultural heritage, language, and history of this country.

During the war, the China-Burma-India Theater was considered a "Pauper's Theater" in terms of military support and political concern.[2] After the defeat of Germany in May 1945, the Allies concentrated on the military problems of winning the war against Japan. At the same time, however, American diplomats continued to stress plans

---

[1] Maurice Matloff, *Strategic Planning For Coalition Warfare, 1943–1944* (Washington: Department of the Army, 1959), pp. 9, 398, 543; and Louis Morton, "Germany First: The Basic Concept of Allied Strategy in World War II," in Kent R. Greenfield (ed.), *Command Decisions* (Washington: Department of the Army, 1960), pp. 11–47.

[2] Theodore White (ed.) *The Stilwell Papers* (New York: Sloane, 1948), p. 156.

dealing with postwar political and economic problems of Europe. Thus at the Potsdam Conference, as Feis points out "while the heads of state were absorbed in the attempt to adjust their ideas about the settlement of Europe, Far Eastern matters were left for the staff to study."[3]

After the war was over, the predominance of the European experts in the State Department over the Asian specialists was virtual assurance that Washington would continue to pay primary attention toward Europe. It was there that the State Department felt that the expansion of Soviet power was most dangerous. Europe alone had a highly developed economic and industrial base and thus the capability of absorbing and effectively utilizing United States aid. Asia, on the other hand, was mainly agrarian and seemed almost helplessly backward. Furthermore, Asia was in the throes of nationalist upheavals. The colonial empires were disintegrating and anti-Western sentiment was widespread. In addition, China, the largest country of Asia, was being ravaged by a bloody civil war. In Asia, therefore, it seemed virtually impossible to try to restore the status quo.

When the war ended in the Pacific, Southeast Asia was given next to lowest priority in Asian affairs by the State Department. Japan, China, and the Philippines (in that order) were considered "more urgent" than Southeast Asia, with only Australasia receiving lower priority. A major reason given for the low priority of Southeast Asia was that countries in this area, with the exception of Thailand, were "politically tied to one or another of the European powers," with the result that United States influence could only be "indirect rather than direct."[4]

Since the State Department placed less importance on Asia than on Europe, and less importance on Southeast

---

[3] Feis, *The China Tangle,* (New York, Atheneum, 1965), p. 324.
[4] U.S. Department of State, Office of Strategic Services, Research and Analysis Branch, R&A No. 3315, *Program of Geographic Work Fundamental to Far East Problems,* August 18, 1945.

Asia than the rest of Asia, it may be deduced that developments in Vietnam received very low priority. There are several additional factors, however, which explain the relatively low priority of Vietnam. First, as mentioned previously, President Truman was not so vehemently opposed to the reimposition of French control over Vietnam as his predecessor.[5] A second factor, also pointed out previously, was that de facto United States recognition of Indo-China as under the British SEAC paved the way for the Potsdam decision which allowed the British to occupy southern Vietnam and thereby soften the area for the return of the French. Thus the United States could not exercise significant postwar influence in Vietnam which she might otherwise have done if Indo-China had remained under General Wedemeyer's command as originally planned.[6]

A third factor was that rapid postwar demobilization of American armed forces rendered it almost impossible for the United States to take forceful action in Vietnam. By the end of October 1945, all American military men comprising only a few small army liaison teams, had left Vietnam, except for a small group with General Gallagher.[7] A final factor was that after Japan was defeated, there seemed to be no serious threat to American interests in Southeast Asia. In Vietnam, the United States Government did not immediately perceive Ho Chi Minh and the Viet Minh as dangerous forces of Communist imperialism.

The American Assessment in the Field of Ho Chi Minh and the Viet Minh, 1944-1945

The United States Government had to consider many

---

[5] See pp. 88–94.

[6] See pp. 71–72.

[7] For details of evacuation of American troops from Vietnam, see Gallagher's letters to McClure, October 16 and 25, 1945, in the Gallagher Papers.

questions in evaluating Ho Chi Minh, but perhaps the most important was whether Ho was more a Communist or a nationalist leader. Whichever was the case, what is useful for our purposes is to recount the United States assessment of Ho's political loyalties because decisions were made on this basis.

The American postwar assessment of Ho was based largely on America's wartime relationship with Ho, particularly that of the OSS. There was a mutual attraction based on one overriding concern—defeat of the Japanese. According to Robert Shaplen, who was a reporter in Indo-China for *Newsweek* during the war, Ho first started to look for American help in the later half of 1944. He saw the OSS as the chief potential source of military supplies and political aid, and the OSS considered Ho and his guerrillas the most effective force of opposition to the Japanese.[8]

There is considerable controversy over the extent of OSS aid to Ho before the conclusion of the war. Shaplen writes that four different times, in late 1944 and in early 1945, Ho secretly went to the OSS in Kunming to ask for arms and ammunition. In return, Ho promised the OSS intelligence aid, anti-Japanese sabotage, and continued assistance in rescuing Allied pilots shot down in the jungle. According to Paul E. Helliwell, who was then chief of OSS in China, Ho's requests for aid were turned down. Helliwell told Shaplen that "OSS China was at all times consistent in its policy of giving no help to individuals such as Ho, who were known Communists and therefore obvious postwar sources of trouble." Helliwell insisted that the original OSS decision not to give arms to Ho was "principally based . . . on Ho's refusal to pledge that any arms he received

---

[8] Robert Shaplen, *The Lost Revolution* (New York: Harper, 1966), p. 33. This is a reliable account of events in Vietnam after World War II, based largely on the author's own experience in the country and documents and interviews given him by Vietnamese and American officials.

would be used only against the Japanese and not against the French."[9]

On the other hand, Helliwell informed Shaplen that he himself was unaware of any direct orders not to help Ho. After initial refusals, Helliwell finally gave Ho six .38 caliber revolvers and twenty thousand rounds of ammunition, but he stated that this was done simply to return a favor for Viet Minh aid in rescuing three American pilots.[10]

According to Shaplen, Ho later wrote to Richard Heppner, who was chief of OSS in China near the end of the war, requesting political as well as military aid. Ho had been greatly impressed by the pledge of the United States to grant the Philippines their freedom after the war, and he hoped that the United States could exert pressure on France to make the same pledge to Vietnam. Shaplen concludes that Ho did receive some additional military aid, from the OSS and other American and Allied agencies, but that "the material aid was not as great as the inspirational encouragement he was unofficially accorded."[11]

Most Americans who had contact with Ho during the war were impressed by Ho as an individual, and particularly by his fanatic patriotism. Shaplen quotes an unidentified American who was with Ho at his jungle headquarters during the war as remembering most Ho's "strength of character and his single-mindedness."[12] Similar American judgments on Ho were related at a special State Department conference on Asia, held in October 1949. At this conference, Mr. J. M. Murphy, a banker, who was in China during the war, recalled that his intelligence unit had spent about two years with Ho, and at least one member had had six months of constant contact with Ho in the jungle. Murphy stated that those who had close contact with Ho in-

[9] Ibid.
[10] Ibid.
[11] Ibid., p. 34.
[12] Ibid.

sisted "that he was at least ninety percent patriot; that they didn't believe that his ties with Russia were the predominant motivation in his life."[13]

After the war was over, the OSS maintained a similar position on Ho. Perhaps the most complete official OSS assessment of Ho can be seen in the following official report made by Major Archimedes Patti, head of OSS in Indo-China, on September 16, 1945:

> . . . Has unquestioned party [Viet Minh] leadership and authority. No other figure in the party approaches any noticeable position of authority.
>
> . . . .
>
> Was approached by General Chennault in 1943 to assist in the recovering of U. S. POW in Indo-China. Worked with AGAS and later with OSS, furnishing intelligence and conducting guerrilla warfare. Is regarded as a real soldier, and his efforts against the Japanese forces as effective.
>
> Is popular with the U. S. Govt. because of his genuine efforts against the Japs. [Near the end of the war] the arms in the hands of his followers were furnished by the U. S. Govt., and not by the Japs as frequently reported.
>
> Is pro-American and violently anti-French. Members of his immediate family have been incarcerated and maltreated at the hands of the French.
>
> Is believed sincere in his political motives, and anxious to cooperate with the Americans.[14]

Ho Chi Minh indeed was anxious to cooperate with the United States since he looked to this country as the main source of help to ensure the success of his struggle against the French. Most Viet Minh leaders were grateful for United States help in defeating Japan. As Vo Nguyen Giap, Vietnam's Minister of the Interior, asserted on September 2, 1945, the day the Republic of Vietnam declared its independence:

[13] U.S. Department of State, "Conference on Problems of United States Policy in China," October 6, 7, 8, 1949, pp. 274–275.

[14] Major A. Patti, "Description of situation in Hanoi and Indo-China generally," September 16, 1945, in the Gallagher Papers.

. . . We have had particularly intimate relations [with the U.S.] which it is for me a pleasant duty to dwell on. . . . The United States of America is a Republic which has no territorial interests in this country. They have paid the greatest contribution to the Vietnamese fight against fascist Japan, our enemy, and so the great American Republic is a good friend of ours.[15]

The Viet Minh expected United States support to continue in its drive for independence from France. Most Vietnamese were impressed by the wealth and prosperity of the United States and thus sought American advice on virtually all aspects of governmental operations[16] The main reason, however, why the Vietnamese looked to the United States was that this country was best able to help them achieve independence. The Vietnamese admired the American revolutionary heritage and democratic tradition

---

[15] Quoted in Allan B. Cole (ed.), *Conflict in Indo-China and International Repercussions, A Documentary History, 1945–1955* (Ithaca, N.Y.: Cornell University Press, 1956), p. 26.

[16] This respect for Americans was emphasized by Hale's Report: "Our prowess in the war, our vast production abilities, our progressiveness in technical and social fields—all were known by the Annamites, to a surprising degree. In their blueprint for self-government they envisaged American trade bringing them peacetime products as superlative as the planes, tanks, and guns they know have won the war in the East, American technicians to help them industrialize Vietnam, American consultants in the political, medical and social sciences. Essentially, they feel that the French did not develop the resources of the country for the benefit of the people themselves, and in their own planning have emphasized their intention to throw Vietnam open to American commercial penetration. As a matter of practical preference they would like to see the economy of Vietnam geared to our own if that were possible or desirable to us. . . . Annamites asked for all sorts of advice—how to run a newspaper, how to repair and operate machinery, how to run a street-cleaning department most efficiently—even though they were managing quite well indeed in operating utilities and other physical functions of government. They inquired about our schools, our courts, our elections, about the workings of both houses of Congress. They seemed to feel that every American contained within himself all the virtues and accomplishments of the nation they wanted most to emulate. *Op. cit.*, pp. 14–15.

and considered the United States alone amongst the Allies as a genuine supporter of independence, not only for Vietnam but for all Asia as well. They were impressed by the role the United States played in generating the Atlantic Charter, and they considered the United States promise of complete independence for the Philippines as proof of her good intentions.[17]

Vietnamese admiration for the United States was strikingly expressed in the Declaration of Independence of the Republic of Vietnam, signed on Steptember 2, 1945. This document was deliberately patterned after the United States Declaration of Independence in content, wording, and style. Vietnam's Declaration begins:

> "All men are created equal. They are endowed by their Creator with certain inalienable rights, among these Life, Liberty, and the Pursuit of Happiness."
> This immortal statement was made in the Declaration of Independence of the United States of America in 1776. . . .[18]

This copying of the American Declaration of Independence was primarily pragmatic. As Ho Chi Minh remarked to Arthur Hale, Vietnam modeled its Declaration of Independence on that of the United States because his people looked to the United States "as the one nation most likely to be sympathetic to our cause."[19] In order to win Ameri-

---

[17] Particularly noteworthy in this regard is Owen Lattimore's observation at the close of the war: "America has at present the clearest power of attraction for all Asia. We have a unique reputation for good faith, because we not only promised freedom to the Philippines but set a date for that freedom. For this one reason our liberation policy is accepted as genuine, while the vague promises to other colonies of "self-government" or "dominion status," at some time in an unspecified future, but not freedom in one word, are subject to the discount of an obstinate suspicion." See *Solution in Asia* (Boston: Little, Brown, 1945), p. 152.

[18] Quoted in Cole, *op. cit.*, pp. 19–21.

[19] Quoted in Hale's Report, *op. cit.*, p. 10.

can support, Ho even went so far as to sound out the possibility of an American trusteeship over Vietnam.[20]

_____

[20] United States Army, MS, "History of the China Theater," *op. cit.*, Chap. V, pp. 34, 40. Wedemeyer feels that this request was never taken seriously by the United States. See Wedemeyer's letter to author, January 30, 1967. The Viet Minh, both shortly before and shortly after its seizure of power, evidently sent out several "feelers" indicating possible postwar political settlements for Vietnam. One such feeler was transmitted through the OSS to the French Government in July 1945. In an aide-memoire, written both in French and in English and thus presumably for American as well as French consumption, the Viet Minh suggested that the future of Vietnam might develop after the war along the following lines:

"1. A parliament will be chosen by universal suffrage. It will legislate for the country. A French Governor will serve as President until independence is secured. This President will choose a Cabinet or a group of advisers accepted by the parliament. The precise powers of all these organs will be settled at a point in the future.

"2. Independence will be given to this country in a minimum of five years and a maximum of ten.

"3. The natural resources of this country will be returned to its inhabitants after an equitable compensation by the current rulers. France will benefit from economic advantages.

"4. All the liberties proclaimed by the United Nations will be guaranteed to the Indo-Chinese.

"5. The sale of opium will be prohibited.

"We hope that these conditions will be judged acceptable by the French Government."

Cited by Philippe Devillers, *op. cit.*, p. 134. It is interesting to point out that the recommendations of the Viet Minh were in accordance with the provisions on colonies in the recently signed United Nations Charter.

Another "feeler" was picked up by the OSS in China shortly after V-J Day. The OSS reported that according to a "representative of the Central Committee in Hanoi," the Viet Minh wanted to make sure that the United States Government knew that Indo-China wanted its independence and had asked Washington to assist by:

    (1) Prohibiting or not aiding the French to enter Indo-China.
    (2) Keeping the Chinese under control to prevent looting and pillaging.
    (3) Sending technical advisors to aid in exploiting resources.
    (4) Developing industries.
    (5) Granting to Indo-China the same status as the Philippines for an indefinite period.

If United States help for independence were not forth-coming, however, Ho suggested that he would be forced to look to the Soviet Union. Colonel Stephen Nordlinger, head of the United States Military Government group in Hanoi, has explained, for instance, that when he lunched with Ho on the last day of his Vietnam mission, Ho emphasized the urgency of American aid. If it did not come, Ho implied that he would have to seek aid from the Soviet Union.[21]

Hale's report in the fall of 1945 suggested that from the very beginning Ho looked not only to the United States but also to the Soviet Union. According to Hale, it was "likely that Ho Chi Minh expected at least as much support from the Soviet as from the United States in what he expected would be an international forum of mediation" to bring about Vietnam's independence.[22] Ho thus was thinking in terms of a continuation of the war-time Soviet-American alliance, and since both countries espoused self-determination, it seemed logical to expect their support. Ho Chi Minh and the Viet Minh, therefore, seemed in the fall of 1945 to have been influenced by the ideologies of both the Soviet Union and the United States.

Hale observed that there was a "considerable communist influence in Viet Minh."[23] His observation is consonant

---

See OSS message from Colonel William P. Davis to Mr. Ellis Briggs, Minister and Counselor, American Embassy, Chungking, August 21, 1945, in the Patrick J. Hurley Collection.

[21] Author's interview with Nordlinger.

[22] Hale's Report, op. cit., p. 10.

[23] Hale observed further: "The flag of Vietnam which it [the Viet Minh] created is a modification of the Soviet flag. The national salute is very nearly the raised right arm salute of communists. Posters, banners, have been adapted from western leftist art. In the main offices of the government young officials have copies of Marxist pamphlets on their desks. But at the same time there is ample evidence of an equally strong influence from the United States. The American experience in the Philippines has been brought to the people, down to the smallest village, by radio and newspaper. Policy statements and declarations by the government

with a decree published in late August 1945 by the Congress of the Indo-Chinese Communist Party (ICP), which read in part:

> . . . We must attract to our side the Soviet Union and the United States, because we shall then be able to offer resistance to the encroachments of the French, who intend to reestablish their former position in Indo-China, and also to the manouvers of certain Chinese militarists, who want to annex our country. . . .[24]

It is important to note that the ICP was dissolved on November 11, 1945. There were many reasons, national, and international, for the dissolution, but one of the most important, according to conjecture by the State Department, was to convince the United States that the Vietnam independence movement was not controlled by the Soviet Union.[25] The dissolution of the ICP, however, did not mean the dissolution of Vietnamese Communism. An Association for the Study of Marxism was formed almost immediately in which Vietnamese Communists could carry on their activities.[26]

From the analysis above, it seems evident that the United States Government in the fall of 1945 had a clear policy choice in Vietnam: whether to help the French regain control or to help Ho Chi Minh establish the independence of Vietnam.

---

are obvious imitations of American techniques of democratic government. In short, the Viet Minh leadership seems to have used communist methods of appeal, revolutionary education and agitation to arouse the masses behind a program for an independent democracy." *Ibid.*, p. 11.

[24] Quoted in Rima Rathausky (ed), *Documents of the August 1945 Revolution* (Canberra: Dept. of International Relations, Research School of Pacific Studies, the Australian National University 1963). These documents were first published in Hanoi in 1959.

[25] U. S. Dept. of State, *Political Alignments of Vietnamese Nationalists,* OIR Report No. 3708, October 1, 1949, p. 92.

[26] See Tran Ngoc Hung, "The Role of the Indochinese Communist Party in the Evolution of the Viet Minh, 1945 to 1951," *The Australian Quarterly,* XXVI (September, 1954), pp. 87–98.

Washington's Policy toward Vietnam in the Fall of 1945

The basic difficulty the United States faced in Vietnam after the war was part of a general postwar dilemma summed up by the historian Julius Pratt:

> Traditionally, it sympathized with peoples seeking independence. Furthermore, it seemed clear that old-fashioned colonialism was dead, that the aspirants for independence made the "wave of the future," and that to oppose them might drive them into the Communist camp. On the other hand, besides harboring some skepticism about the capacity of inexperienced nationalities for self-government, the United States could ill afford to antagonize its European allies by helping divest them of their valued overseas possessions.[27]

Joseph Ballantine, special assistant to Secretary of State Byrnes, made the following comment on this dilemma in the Fall of 1945:

> We have to think not only of our relations with Asiatic peoples but of our relations with the Europeans. There is a balance which we have to strike there. We need the good will of France and the Netherlands and Great Britain. So I think we have to be very circumspect.[28]

The United States Government resolved this dilemma on the basis of its "Europe first" policy. Washington was sympathetic to the cause of Vietnamese independence, but it considered the economic rehabilitation and political independence of France more important. The United States

---

[27] Julius W. Pratt, "Anticolonialism in United States Policy," in Robert Strausz-Hupé and Harry Hazard (eds.), *The Idea of Colonialism* (New York: Praeger, 1958), pp. 133–134.

[28] Joseph Ballantine, "The Far East," in Quincy Wright (ed.), *A Foreign Policy for the United States* (Chicago: University of Chicago Press, 1947), p. 161. In 1944, Ballantine was Director of the Office of Far Eastern Affairs.

Government espoused the principle of self-determination of all peoples, but supporting the self-determination of France against the threat of Soviet imperialism took priority over supporting self-determination of France's colonies. Since most Frenchmen saw their empire as a symbol of France's strength and unity, the State Department considered support of the French in Vietnam essential for the maintenance of a strong, stable, French government.[29] Edwin Reischauer, who served with the Office of Far Eastern Affairs in the State Department from 1945 to 1946, stresses this point:

> . . . The chief argument for not backing Asian nationalism and for supporting the restoration of the colonial empires was in terms of the problems of the colonial powers in Europe. . . . They had been through a great deal.
> There was, perhaps, the question of political stability in a country like France, and I am sure it was argued we must give them this sort of support because of the situation in Europe.[30]

Official United States policy statements reflect this choice of priorities. In a speech on October 20, 1945, for instance, John Carter Vincent, Director of the Office of Far Eastern Affairs in the State Department, quoted a joint statement issued by Chiang Kai-shek and Henry Wallace on June 24, 1944 which advocated

> the recognition of the fundamental right of presently de-

---

[29] The Soviet Union was also caught in the dilemma of whether to support the French or the Vietnamese. Like the United States, the Soviet Union opted for the French in the immediate postwar period. For a good analysis of the Soviet dilemma, see Bernard Fall, "Tribulations of a Party Line, The French Communists and Indo-China," *Foreign Affairs*, XXXIII (April, 1955), pp. 499–510, and Charles B. McLane, *Soviet Strategies in Southeast Asia* (Princeton, N.J.: Princeton University Press, 1966).

[30] *Asia, the Pacific, and the United States.* Hearings Before the Committee on Foreign Relations, U. S. Senate, 90th Cong., 1st Sess. (Washington: G.P.O., 1967), p. 53.

pendent Asiatic peoples to self-government and the adoption of measures, in the political, economic, and social fields to *prepare* these peoples for *self-government* within a specified practical limit [my italics].

Vincent then quoted Cordell Hull's statement of March 12, 1944, which stressed

the duty of nations having political ties with [colonies] . . . to help aspiring peoples to develop materially and educationally to *prepare* themselves for the responsibilities of *self-government*, and to attain liberty [my italics].

He then added:

It is not our intention to assist or participate in forceful measures for the reimposition of control by the territorial sovereigns. . . .

In the same breath, however, Vincent remarked:

. . . with regard to the situation in French Indo-China, this government does not question French sovereignty in that area.[31]

Vincent's speech was given widely different interpretations by the French and the Vietnamese. According to Hale's report, Vincent's statement "was apparently all things to all factions in Indo-China." The Annamese press reported it under the headline, "U.S. Recognizes Independency of Vietnam," and the French in their daily news bulletin hailed it with "America Upholds French Sovereignty in Indo-China."[32] The French rather than the Vietnamese, however, seemed to have interpreted Vincent's remarks correctly. The Vietnamese press, therefore, seems either to have misinterpreted Vincent's remarks because of wishful thinking, or more likely perhaps, to have deliber-

[31] *DSB,* October 21, 1945, pp. 644–646.
[32] Hale's Report, *op. cit.,* p. 15.

ately played up his remarks regarding independence for domestic propaganda value.

One week later, on October 27, 1945, President Truman delivered a speech in which he too dealt with the problem of independence for colonial peoples. Truman stated:

> We believe in the *eventual* return of sovereign rights and *self-government* to all peoples who have been deprived of them by force. . . .
> We believe that all peoples who are prepared for self-government should be permitted to choose their own form of government by their own freely expressed choice without interference from any foreign source. That is true in Europe, in Asia, in Africa, as well as in the Western Hemisphere.
>
> . . . .
>
> We shall refuse to recognize any government imposed upon any nation by the force of any foreign power . . . [my italics].[33]

It is important that Truman did not speak of *immediate* independence for all colonies, but of the "eventual" return of sovereignty and "self-government." Truman, like Vincent, had chosen his words carefully. They were in strict accordance with the Dumbarton Oaks Agreement and the United Nations Charter, and thus did not rule out the possibility of a French protectorate over Vietnam. The United States, therefore, would let France decide what policy was best for the future of Vietnam.

Another indication that the United States would give France a free hand in regaining control over Vietnam was a statement by Secretary of State James Byrnes on October 24, 1945. When Byrnes was asked at a press conference about the use of American lend-lease armament by the British and Dutch against the Indonesians, he replied that the United States Government maintained a "hands off" policy toward all conflicts involving nationalist revolution-

---

[33] *DSB*, October 28, 1945, pp. 653–656.

aries against colonial forces. He added, however, that the United States was against the use of American insignia on lend-lease military equipment "in circumstances that would produce political complications" for her. Byrnes then announced that he had asked all colonial authorities to remove American insignia from all equipment used for political purposes. When newsmen asked the Secretary whether the United States should not demand the return of this equipment, Byrnes replied weakly that this was a matter of contracts about which he knew very little. Byrnes then made a comment which dealt generally with the lend-lease equipment problem and which had important implications for American policy in Vietnam:

> Whether anything will be done toward having lend-lease equipment returned to us appears to be highly improbable in view of the difficulties that would be encountered with a government that wished to retain the armament.[34]

Byrnes implied, therefore, that the United States would not press France to return lend-lease supplies.[35]

The use of American lend-lease military equipment after the war by the European colonial powers to recover their colonies was decried one month later by Ambassador Patrick Hurley, who was a bitter critic of American policy in the Far East. Since he could not resolve his difficulties with Washington, Hurley resigned his post. In his letter of resignation to President Truman on November 26, 1945, Hurley sharply condemned what he considered the choice

---

[34] *New York Times,* October 25, 1945, p. 4.

[35] Harold Isaacs points out that in southern Vietnam, in the early fall of 1945, "French troops were arriving, thousands every week, first in French transports and then in a long succession of American ships, flying the American flag and manned by American crews. They came ashore in their American uniforms, with their American lend-lease weapons—tanks, trucks, jeeps," *op cit.* p. 161. The use of American vessels to transport French troops to Saigon and the damage to U.S. prestige in the eyes of Vietnamese caused thereby is also cited in Hale's Report, *op. cit.,* p. 21.

by the United States Government of European colonialism over Asian nationalism. He explained:

> The astonishing feature of our foreign policy is the wide discrepancy between our announced policies and our conduct of international relations. For instance, we began the war with the principles of the Atlantic Charter and democracy as our goal. . . . We finished the war in the Far East furnishing lend-lease supplies and using all our reputation to undermine democracy and bolster imperialism. . . .[36]

In Vietnam itself, official American non-interventionist policy soon became official American diplomatic support for the French, at least indirectly. This was obfuscated, however, because there were three main American groups in north Vietnam, each operating independently. There was the Military Advisory and Assistance Group (MAAG) under General Philip Gallagher, whose general function was to help the Chinese with the occupation. Also present was the Military Government Group (G-5) under Colonel Stephen Nordlinger, whose main task was to effect the release, rehabilitation, and eventual repatriation of all allied prisoners of war. The third group was the OSS under Major Archimedes Patti, whose assignment was to make preparations for the Japanese surrender.[37]

MAAG, G-5, and the OSS operated simultaneously in north Vietnam but not always in unison or in concert.

---

[36] "The Ambassador to China (Hurley) to President Truman," Annex no. 50, in Department of State, *United States Relations with China* (Washington: G.P.O. 1949), pp. 581-584.

[37] A fourth group of Americans, the Air-Ground-Aid Service (AGAS) was also present in north Vietnam located just outside Hanoi. AGAS continued its wartime assignment on a very limited basis of helping recover and treat Allied pilots downed in flights between China and Vietnam. The communication facilities of AGAS, particularly the radio to Shanghai, were especially valuable to MAAG and G-5 for requesting supplies. AGAS will not be analyzed further because of its relatively minor importance during the Allied occupation period.

What their policies were and how they were determined will now be examined.

The Policy of the Military Advisory and Assistance Group

At the end of the war, approximately 3,200,000 Japanese were scattered throughout Korea, China (particularly Manchuria) and Indo-China. About two million of these Japanese were civilians, many of whom were not born in Japan and had never even been in their homeland. Slightly over one million were soldiers who had fought the Allies. After V-J Day, General Wedemeyer, the China Theater commander, was directed by the JCS to facilitate the repatriation of these Japanese. This was a task of great magnitude and complexity, which required meticulous planning, preparation, and coordination. To execute this operation, Wedemeyer sent out groups of Chinese and Americans to the various parts of the China Theater.

General Gallagher was Senior Adviser in charge of the American group sent to Indo-China, which arrived on September 14, 1945. Gallagher's original directive, dated August 24, 1945, was

> to assist and advise the Chinese in the rapid occupation of [Indo-China] and to act as Staff Officer to the Chinese Commander in the surrender of, and assist in the disposition of the Japanese forces, and to liberate and rehabilitate Allied internees and prisoners of war, and to render U.S. medical assistance in emergency care of these individuals now in Japanese hands.[38]

It must be pointed out that nothing in this order indicated that Gallagher's mission was to facilitate the re-establishment of French control of Vietnam. The only part of

---

[38] Letter from General Gallagher to author, January 5, 1967.

the directive which applied to the French was that dealing with the liberation and rehabilitation of French prisoners of war. MAAG thus was not originally intended to be a political group in any way and was in fact admonished not to become involved in fratricidal or internecine struggles.[39] Gallagher was not told whom he was to support politically, nor was he given any guidance indicating that he was to work for or channel his activities towards the re-establishment of French control. Thus when Gallagher arrived, he tried to avoid getting involved in political issues since he lacked a directive authorizing him to do so. Gallagher observed, however, that "despite this, political significance was read into everything I or my group did of an official nature or social routine; our activities or utterances were often twisted or magnified positively or negatively, to suit the purpose of the faction involved."[40]

The major reason for this predicament was the competing demands made upon Gallagher's group by the Vietnamese, French, and Chinese. Most of Gallagher's dealings with the Vietnamese were through Ho Chi Minh. Contrary to the conclusion of Bernard Fall,[41] Gallagher knew very well the Communist background of Ho,[42] but he "dealt with him because there was no one else to deal with with any authority, or sense of responsibility."[43] Ho himself, from the very beginning, tried to get on the good side of Gallagher who, he felt, was empowered to act politically. When Gallagher and his men arrived in Hanoi, they saw strung across a main street a large red and gold banner which read: "Welcome Liberators." Accordingly, Ho provided these Americans with a very comfortable and beautiful

---

[39] Letter from General Albert Wedemeyer to author, January 19, 1967; letter from General Robert McClure, Commanding General, Chinese Combat Command, to author, January 15, 1967.
[40] Gallagher's Brief, undated, in the Gallagher Papers.
[41] Fall, *The Two Vietnams, op. cit.,* p. 207.
[42] Gallagher's letter to McClure, September 20, 1945.
[43] Gallagher's letter to author, *op. cit.*

lake-front home, and put many Vietnamese servants at their disposal. And at Ho's first meeting with Gallagher, the Viet Minh leader "called on me and welcomed us most profusely, gave me a very beautiful red banner with my name on it, and some remark about the "Great American nation," etc. . . ."[44]

Ho's attempts to curry favor with the Americans, however, received periodic setbacks because of unfortunate incidents which were played up by the press. The first such incident caused Ho to rush to the Americans to explain about a particular AP dispatch from Saigon which read as follows:

> The rioting Annamese killed one American officer, wounded another, and besieged U.S. headquarters one hour Wednesday in the first incident involving U.S. forces in Indo-China.
> Colonel Peter Dewey was killed by a machine gun bullet while he was attempting to pass the Annamite territory in a short automobile drive from the local airfield to his headquarters. The Annamites then attacked Colonel Dewey's headquarters and injured several more persons.[45]

Ho immediately expressed his "profound regret" that this incident occurred, and he assured General Gallagher that such an incident would occur in the area "only over my dead body." Ho then explained that he believed the incident might have been staged by the French, yet he also admitted sadly that "it might have been the action of unruly elements of the Annamese." Ho concluded that "such actions could in the long run only hurt the cause" for which he was striving, and "lessen the regard" in which

---

[44] Gallagher's letter to McClure, September 20, 1945. General Gallagher later presented this banner to the U.S. Army Counter-Intelligence Corps Museum at Fort Holabird, Maryland.

[45] Quoted in Memorandum for the Record, Headquarters-Forward Echelon I Army Group Command Chinese Combat Command (Prov) United States Forces China Theater, September 29, 1945, in the Gallagher Papers.

the Annamese people were held by the outside world. Finally Ho stated that he would write a letter to the State Department "deploring the occurrence and expressing regret, and also, explaining the situation regarding the occurrence from the Annamese viewpoint, as clearly as possible."[46]

It is evident, therefore, that Ho, in his attempts to win favor from General Gallagher, misunderstood the nature and function of MAAG's mission. This is clearly brought out by General Gallagher, who wrote that he gleaned the following impression from his few meetings with Ho:

> I am sure that he and his followers thought my "U.S. Liaison Group" with General Lu Han's Army Group, was a full-blown Allied "Commission" empowered to accomplish far more than the disarming of Japanese troops. They planned for our arrival and greeted and treated us accordingly.
> . . . . He was, I am sure, disappointed when it was pointed out to him that we could do nothing officially (at government level) to help his cause and that our primary function was to advise the Chinese Army and assist in maintaining law and order.

Ho even requested that Gallagher send messages to Washington for him. Gallagher refused, although he did accept and dispatch through regular channels a sealed letter ad-

---

[46] *Ibid.* According to the evidence examined by this author, the only official U.S. presence in southern Vietnam during the postwar occupation period was a very small group of OSS men under Colonel Dewey. Little is known of their activities either before or after Dewey's death. Colonel Nordlinger suggests that Dewey's assignment in the area may have been the same as his in the north (see *infra,* p. 141). Author's interview with Nordlinger, November 15, 1968. General Gallagher disagrees, conjecturing that Dewey and his men were doing intelligence work. Gallagher's letter to author, January 10, 1969. Whatever the case, this guesswork as to Dewey's activities indicates a serious lack of policy coordination and communication between the Americans above and below the 16th parallel.

dressed to President Truman. This author has found no evidence that Ho ever received a reply.[47]

In the first few days that Gallagher was in Vietnam, he concentrated on helping the Chinese execute their occupation duties. Gallagher's main dealings with Lu Han concerned the treatment of the French by the Chinese. Gallagher felt that Lu Han was naturally sympathetic toward the Vietnamese and hated the French. One of Gallagher's major tasks, therefore, in keeping with the political neutrality of his mission, was to insist that Lu Han treat the French and Vietnamese alike. Gallagher was thus continually "acting as a neutral go-between."[48]

Perhaps the most important issue that concerned General Gallagher was whether the Chinese were to work for the re-establishment of French control in north Vietnam. As stated previously, Gallagher had been directed on August 24, 1945 to be politically neutral. There is evidence, however, that during the third week in September both Gallagher and Lu Han were ordered by the China Combat Command to help the French. Reference to this new order is seen in a letter of September 27 from Gallagher to General Robert McClure, his immediate superior in China, which opens:

> Very little change in the situation here since my last letter report [on September 20]. The most important one was the

[47] A telegram of October 18, 1945 from Ho Chi Minh to President Truman, summarizing the text of a letter of September 29, 1945 from Ho to Truman, is located in the Department of State files. Unfortunately, these messages are still classified. A broadcast by Radio Hanoi on October 15, however, reveals that Ho's letter to Truman stated that when France "handed over the reins of the Government [of Vietnam] to Japan" in March 1945 and "betrayed the Allies," she lost her right to sit on an "Allied Advisory Commission" which Ho felt would decide the postwar status of Vietnam. Ho then asked Truman to allow Vietnam to sit on this Advisory Commission.

[48] Gallagher's Brief, *op. cit.*

message in which you indicated that the Chinese were to facilitate the recovery of power by the French.[49]

Gallagher immediately informed the French Generals who were "overjoyed and expected to go from rags to riches overnight." General Alessandri, one of de Gaulle's official representatives in Hanoi, immediately contacted Lu Han and asked him "to rearm all French immediately, take back all of the public utilities and the houses of former French officials, particularly for himself, so he would gain face, etc." Gallagher maintained that all of Alessandri's requests were "proper under the new conditions," but that Lu Han had refused to offer any aid until he "got orders from Ho Ying Chin (Lu's commander) on the new deal."[50]

When the Viet Minh leaders sensed the change in American policy, they were very disappointed. This disappointment was reflected, for instance, in a change in the Viet Minh's treatment of American soldiers. Gallagher reported on September 27:

There has been a noticeable change in the attitude of the Annamites towards the Americans here in Hanoi since they became aware of the fact that we were not going to interfere and would probably help the French. Some of our officers, who were previously welcomed with open arms at Viet Minh headquarters are now permitted to cool their heels indefinitely and are sometimes refused audiences with certain members of the Viet Minh government. How far this antagonism will go on the part of the Viet Minh, I don't know. . . .[51]

Gallagher asserts that his headquarters, which had its own communications, definitely received this new order.

[49] Gallagher's letter to McClure, September 27, 1945.
[50] Ibid.
[51] Ibid. Gallagher does not believe that Ho and other Viet Minh leaders "knew that a new directive was promulgated in late September," but that "they began to back away from us when they found that we were not going to actively support their desire to eliminate the French." Gallagher's letter to author, January 5, 1967.

When he confronted Lu Han with this new directive to help the French, however, the Chinese General was "very much surprised" and "pleaded ignorance." Gallagher suggests that Lu was trying "to stall for time and actually avoid helping the French," so "he fell back on the excuse that he did not have any new orders from his Hq."[52] Gallagher then requested McClure to get Ho Ying Chin to give him some specific orders to help the French. About September 30, General McClure and General Ho Ying Chin came to Hanoi and it may have been at this time that this matter was straightened out between the Chinese commanders concerned.

General Gallagher, in accordance with his new directive, began to influence Lu Han to help the French regain control of North Vietnam. In a conference with Lu on October 25, Gallagher reported, he "finally got him [Lu] to agree that he should not hinder French efforts and should meet their requests where possible." Gallagher continued that although Lu insisted that he had received

> no word that he should facilitate their activities, he agreed with me that eventually the French would regain control of this area and it would be to his best interest not to have hampered their activities too much. To date, he has given them damned little, but I have hopes he will turn over a new leaf after our conference yesterday. At least he assured me he would.

Gallagher reported further that he realized that the removal of Japanese troops from Indo-China had "a very low priority on MacArthur's schedule," yet he was wary that French-Annamese animosity might soon flare up into open war. Gallagher concluded, therefore, that

---

[52] *Ibid.* It is important to note that Philippe Devillers also alludes to this change in official U.S. policy toward support of France. According to Devillers, in October the U.S. State Department "seemed to give assurances to France, disavowing more or less the policy of the OSS [which had been favoring the Viet Minh]." *Op. cit.,* p. 203.

the smartest thing Wedemeyer could do would be to urge
the early removal of Japanese from the area occupied by
Lu Han, so that Lu Han could pull his troops out of the
picture, *permitting the French a free hand in settling their
score with the Annamites . . .* [my italics].[53]

As has been already indicated, however, the Chinese
did not agree to withdraw their troops until February
1946.[54] In the meantime, Lu Han did nothing to help the
French regain political control. As Gallagher asserted:
"there was no action . . . that indicated that the Chinese
[tried] to put the French "back in the saddle.""[55] Yet despite Galagher's efforts to persuade Lu Han to help the
French, and Lu Han's refusal, the two Generals ended
their stay in Vietnam on an ostensibly friendly note. In
response to a warm letter from Gallagher on December
16, 1945, four days after he left Vietnam, Lu Han wrote
back as follows:

In training my army, in preparing the offensive, in accept-
ing the surrender of Japanese in French Indo-China and in
maintaining peace and order over there, I owe you very
much. During your stay with us, you have not only made a
great military and political contribution, but have also
promoted friendly relations between China and the United
States. . . .[56]

Inasmuch as Lu delayed acting upon Gallagher's request
to pull out and let the French take over, Gallagher concentrated on other aspects of his duties. Gallagher did all
he could, for instance, to protect Frenchmen from incensed
Vietnamese who made frequent raids on French billets.

[53] Gallagher's letter to McClure, October 26, 1945.
[54] According to Buttinger, the last Chinese troops did not leave
until June, 1946. See Buttinger, *op. cit.,* I, 369.
[55] Gallagher's letter to author, January 5, 1967.
[56] Letter from Lu Han (then Governor of Yunnan Province) to
General Gallagher, January 3, 1946. A copy of this letter was sent
by Gallagher to author and is not part of the Gallagher Papers.

General Alessandri personally thanked Gallagher for having posted sentries outside his family's home, part of which was used as a French nursery where many French children also stayed at night, after some Vietnamese had entered the premises and terrorized the occupants. "I know that without your action," Alessandri wrote Gallagher, "my family would have continued to suffer ceaseless maltreatment by a few bandits from the Viet Minh."[57] In effect, therefore, General Gallagher's help to the French in Hanoi was mainly physical protection.

Whereas the MAAG team under General Gallagher had been sent to Hanoi, additional MAAG liaison teams under his direction had accompanied Chinese occupation forces into other cities in North Vietnam such as Hue, Haiphong, and Vinh. In Hue, the American liaison team with the Chinese 60th Army was headed by Colonel John Stodter. Along the route to Hue, they found that many French were in the custody of the Viet Minh who were keeping them in "most unsatisfactory conditions." The U.S. liaison team did all it could to influence the Chinese to effect the release of the French and protect them. But the 60th Army was anti-French and at first it tried "to avoid helping the French." But as soon as General Gallagher learned of this situation, he contacted Lu Han who then immediately ordered the release of the French prisoners and their protection from the Vietnamese.[58]

Arriving in Haiphong in the middle of September, the American liaison team under Lieutenant Colonel Maris found a "critical situation . . . existing between the French and Annamites." This MAAG team then "acted promptly in this matter, taking over the guard of the French pris-

---

[57] Letter from General Alessandri to Gallagher, November 26, 1945. A copy of this letter was sent by Gallagher to author and also is not part of the Gallagher Papers.
[58] Gallagher's letter to McClure, October 16, 1945.

oners and the running of the city."[59] Toward the middle
of October, with an improvement in this situation, General Gallagher began frequent visits to Haiphong to prepare for the evacuation from Vietnam to southern China
of both Chinese occupation forces (in areas other than
Hanoi) and of all Americans, except for a skeleton crew
under his command in Hanoi and Haiphong. In these
preparations, Gallagher established a very close relationship with the U.S. Navy off Haiphong under Admiral
Buckmaster, which had arrived on October 16.[60] Most of
these Chinese forces left on American vessels by December,
and all Americans, except the small group with Gallagher,
left by the second week in November. What were the
policies and actions of these Americans, however, before
they left?

The Policy of the Military
Government Group

G-5, commanded by Colonel Nordlinger,[61] was assigned

---

[59] There was also conflict between the Chinese 62nd Army in
Haiphong and local Vietnamese. One report received by General
Gallagher concerned an armed clash in which five Vietnamese and
three Chinese were killed. When Gallagher told Lu Han about this,
the Chinese general was "very resentful," claming that "the 62nd
Army was a source of trouble, that they had come into the country
and were acting as conquerors, taking property from the Annamites
and incurring their animosity." Lu added that he had had a conference with the vice commander of the 62nd Army and had "laid
down strict instructions that they not act as conquerors, but merely
occupy the area peacefully, paying for what they needed." Gallagher's letter to McClure, September 20, 1945.

[60] Gallagher's letter to McClure, October 16, 1945.

[61] Colonel Nordlinger had been one of a group of American
officers training Chinese Nationalist officers in southern China.
Nordlinger was working in Kunming when his new orders came
through General Sultan. Like most other American officers at the
time, Nordlinger had no special knowledge of Vietnam. He was
thus chosen for his mission on other criteria: his outstanding Army
service in both World Wars and his fluency in speaking French.

a principally humanitarian mission. Shortly after V-J Day, Nordlinger was given verbal instructions to take seven officers and thirteen enlisted men to Hanoi to locate, rehabilitate, and eventually evacuate about six thousand Allied prisoners of war. He was told that his mission was "both military and civilian in nature," and that in this connection he was "to do everything possible to secure the humanitarian treatment of all elements of the civil community whether French, Annamite, Indian, Chinese, or any other nationality." He was given $10,000 in Indo-Chinese currency and some Army rations to use for this purpose. Nordlinger was also ordered, as was Gallagher on August 24, 1945, to avoid any political involvement, especially between the French and the Vietnamese.[62]

Colonel Nordlinger and his men flew into the Japanese-held airport outside Hanoi on August 24.[63] The Americans were given two old trucks by the Japanese and then drove into the city. Having been given no specific instructions as to where to stay, the Americans accepted the Japanese suggestion to be quartered in the Hotel Metropole.

When Nordlinger arrived at the hotel, he saw a frightening situation indeed. There were about three hundred French, mostly women and children, living in fear inside the hotel which was surrounded by armed Vietnamese, many brandishing spears in a menacing manner. During his first night at the hotel, Nordlinger was informed by the former French Chief of Police in Hanoi that a massacre of the French in the hotel was imminent. Nordlinger immediately radioed American headquarters in Shanghai for instructions. The answer he received the next day, seemingly totally unrealistic under the circumstances, was,

---

[62] Author's interview with Nordlinger, November 15, 1968.

[63] When Nordlinger's plane landed, it was surrounded by the Japanese who were still in control of the airport and who were not even sure the war had ended. The Japanese accepted Nordlinger's argument, however, that he obviously would not have landed in this manner if the war were not over.

"Use your arms only in defense of American lives." Fortunately there was no such massacre that night or during the rest of Nordlinger's stay in Hanoi, although there were sporadic, wanton Vietnamese attacks on Frenchmen in the streets, especially at night.[64]

In fulfillment of its humanitarian assignment, G-5 tried to alleviate as much as possible the sufferings of Allied prisoners of war and their families. Most of the prisoners (about four thousand)—including not only Frenchmen but also Australians, Indians and legionnaires from many other countries—were incarcerated in the Citadel, a wire enclosed compound. The situation of these prisoners was very deplorable. Under Japanese control until the Viet Minh took over shortly after V-J Day, prisoners in the Citadel were dying at a rate of about ten each night, and most of those who were alive were very emaciated and sickly. Adding to the seriousness of the situation was the fact that the Viet Minh had taken over hospitals from the French and had evicted Allied prisoners to make room for Vietnamese. All the French especially had been ousted from these hospitals, including French doctors and nurses. One of Nordlinger's first tasks, therefore, was to influence Ho Chi Minh to return the hospitals to French medical supervision so that all patients, both Allied prisoners and Vietnamese, would receive better treatment and care. Ho finally agreed and the medical situation greatly improved aided significantly by Nordlinger's provision of large supplies of American medicines.

Good support for Nordlinger's efforts was received from Services of Supply (SOS) in Kunming, which distributed the large amounts of medicine and food. Nordlinger was also aided by another American, Waldron C. White, the only Red Cross man in Hanoi after the war ended.[65] White met

---

[64] Author's interview with Nordlinger, November 15, 1968.

[65] White had been stationed with a U.S. fighter group at the Mengtze Air Force Base in southern China during the war, doing

with Ho Chi Minh about three or four times a week, for Ho sought foodstuffs for his people to alleviate the very bad food shortage. White, asked especially for milk, finally succeeded in having twenty-one tons of U.S. surplus supplies flown into Hanoi to be distributed to all in need. Twelve tons of this was powdered milk, with the rest comfort items such as razor blades, tooth brushes, and combs. Several times, White's late arrival at meetings between Ho and General D'Alessandri caused a cessation of vitriolic exchanges between the two leaders, who accused each other, among other things, of stealing milk supplies. There was no doubt in White's mind that it was his Red Cross badge which calmed them down, for both the French and Vietnamese desperately needed whatever Red Cross supplies White could acquire and distribute. During his mission, White also processed about two thousand personal messages from prisoners of war to their next of kin. It should be stressed, however, that in no way was White's mission political. He was neither informed about political policy nor did he inquire about it.[66]

There seems to have been some doubt, however, at least initially, as to the extent of Colonel Nordlinger's neutrality. General Gallagher, before he received orders to facilitate the reimposition of French control, complained to McClure that Nordlinger was not remaining politically neutral. Thus as Gallagher noted:

> I found that he [Nordlinger] had extended his effort beyond

---

Red Cross work. A few days after the war, White and a few other Americans from the base had flown into Hanoi on their own just to see what the place looked like. The men with White were especially curious to see the effects of their bombings on Japanese transportation facilities in the area. When White arrived in Hanoi, Nordlinger thought he had been sent from Kunming, for the Colonel just prior to White's arrival had requested such aid. White then left Hanoi and returned "officially" a few days later to begin his stay of about seven weeks.

[66] Author's interview with White, November 29, 1968.

that of merely helping the prisoners of war, in that he was carrying the torch wholly and completely for all the French in this area. They have come to him with everyone of their personal problems, and he has sympathized with them and indicated that he would act in their behalf. This, of course, he should not do, because he is not in a position to do it.[67]

Gallagher asserted further that in the first week of MAAG's mission he informed Nordlinger that it was necessary for G-5 to do its job "but in no way carry the torch for either the Annamites or the French." Accordingly, Gallagher explained to Nordlinger that any French claims against the Annamites or Japanese had to be submitted in writing "in the form of affidavits." These had to be presented to Lu Han who then would give them to the persons concerned. If personal or public property was stolen or lost, this problem had to be handled by the War Claims Commission. Nordlinger agreed to follow these procedures as outlined.[68]

From Gallagher's assertions Nordlinger seems to have given the French both humanitarian and political assistance, at least in the early phase of his mission. Nordlinger insists, however, that he remained politically neutral from the time he arrived until he left on October 24, 1945. All evidence available to this author supports this conclusion. One example of Nordlinger's early attempts to remain politically neutral concerns his choice of residence. After a brief stay at the Hotel Metropole, Nordlinger and his men moved to another residence. But when Nordlinger learned that this house had originally belonged to a French family which had collaborated with the Japanese, he immediately informed Ho Chi Minh of his desire to move. Ho thereupon provided Nordlinger with a fine residence in Hanoi, which had been the former home of a Chinese merchant, as well as with a small group of servants.

---

[67] Letter from Gallagher to McClure, September 20, 1945.
[68] *Ibid.*

Regarding the large numbers of Frenchmen who came to Nordlinger for assistance, the Colonel asserts that they frequently drifted into his headquarters reporting their troubles because his mission was humanitarian and because he was sympathetic to their plight, i.e., their defenselessness against wanton Vietnamese attacks on their person and property. Nordlinger explains that relatively few French went to General Gallagher since his duties did not directly involve such matters, nor would they have gone to Major Patti of the OSS since he was outspokenly anti-French politically. Nordlinger maintains that he never offered the French political aid nor did he ever indicate he would act in their behalf politically. However he did make detailed reports of all French allegations of Vietnamese attacks against them and relayed them to Ho Chi Minh, who to some extent tried to prevent further outbreaks of the sort.[69]

Nordlinger suggests, that Gallagher at first may have incorrectly judged his activities as pro-French for several reasons. Besides the fact that Nordlinger spoke French and therefore perhaps seemed more at ease in his discussions with French leaders, he was quite friendly with Jean Sainteny. There was one incident in particular involving Sainteny which may have appeared to Gallagher and others that Nordlinger was helping the French politically. One day, Sainteny had gone out in his car with a French flag waving at the helm. His car was surrounded by a Vietnamese mob which destroyed the flag and dragged him off. The Viet Minh then threw him in jail. Sainteny was released only after Colonel Nordlinger's personal intercession with Ho Chi Minh. According to Nordlinger, this intercession was nonpolitical and in accordance with his mission. Moreover, Nordlinger maintains that his relations with Sainteny were purely personal throughout and

---

[69] Author's interview with Nordlinger, November 15, 1968.

that Sainteny never asked him for any political favor.[70] Nordlinger's friendship may have been particularly disturbing to Gallagher, however, who felt that Sainteny was "the instigator of a lot of propaganda, trying to stir up trouble between the Annamites and ourselves and between the Chinese and the Annamites."[71]

Another reason why Nordlinger's efforts may have been judged pro-French politically was that the Colonel worked hard to restore to French medical supervision hospitals seized by the Viet Minh. To succeed in this, Nordlinger had to win the confidence and respect of Ho Chi Minh. He had almost daily association with Ho and the two men developed a particularly close relationship.[72] Nordlinger was very successful in this task and received high praise from the French. Whatever concessions in behalf of French prisoners and their families Nordlinger gained from Ho, however, were of a humanitarian rather than political nature.[73]

---

[70] *Ibid.*

[71] Letter from Gallagher to McClure, September 20, 1945.

[72] When Nordlinger left Vietnam, Ho presented him with a gift of a beautifully embroidered bird about seven feet long which took three men three days to complete. Ho also gave Nordlinger a sealed envelope containing several letters to be delivered to the State Department when he returned to Washington. These letters, Ho told Nordlinger, were addressed to the President, State Department, American Federation of Labor, and the young people of America. Ho gave Nordlinger no indication of why he sent these letters. No further information is available on these letters. Even Colonel Nordlinger was given no information by the State Department when he later made inquiry.

[73] Author's interview with Nordlinger, November 15, 1968. See also a summary report of events in Vietnam by General de Froissard-Broissia, dated October 15, 1945, which stated in part: "Colonel Nordlinger has always refused to treat questions touching close to or far from policy. But . . . without a doubt fixed by his instructions, his action has tended constantly to improve the lot of former prisoners and even to bring assistance in whatever way possible to their families." Colonel Nordlinger was also cited for his frequent intervention in behalf of the French in the following matters: occupation of French houses by Chinese, arrests of French by the

Thus it seems that Gallagher, at the outset, may have misconstrued Nordlinger's thoroughness in performing his humanitarian mission as political aid to the French. Whatever doubt Gallagher had about the politics of Nordlinger's mission, however, seems to have been dispelled by the time Nordlinger concluded his mission. In a special commendation for his work, Gallagher praised Nordlinger for doing an outstanding job while avoiding political involvement.[74]

Whereas Nordlinger's mission was essentially apolitical, this was not the case with another group of Americans in Vietnam, the OSS, which was anti-French.

The Policy of the OSS

OSS Indo-China has been the subject of considerable controversy. It has been both highly praised and vilified. As most of the OSS documents are not yet available, OSS activities can only be interpolated from information which is available.

The OSS was the first American group to arrive in Hanoi. A few OSS officers parachuted into the city on August 22, 1945. They were escorted to the center of Hanoi by the Japanese and were quartered in the Hotel Metropole. Through the communication facilities of this OSS group, preliminary negotiations for the Japanese surrender in Hanoi were conducted, and arrangements were made for

---

Viet Minh, and Chinese searches in the French Camp. This report is located in Colonel Nordlinger's personal files.

[74] See Commendation of October 24, 1945, in Colonel Nordlinger's personal files, in which General Gallagher stated in part: "Your work was often handicapped and complicated by the critical political situation existing between the Annamites and the French. Your complete understanding of the political situation and your common sense methods and finesse in handling the involved problems reflects great credit upon your ability and that of your subordinates."

the entry into Hanoi of the Chinese occupation forces and MAAG.[75]

Since the specific operations of the OSS were mostly unknown to outsiders, numerous rumors have cropped up and allegations made which may or may not reflect the truth. There are numerous examples of French allegations that the OSS gave support to the Viet Minh against the reassertion of French control over Vietnam. Fall, for instance, points out that Pierre Messmer, France's newly appointed Commissioner for northern Indo-China and France's Defense Minister since 1960, was one of the senior officers parachuted from an American C-47 into Vietnam shortly before V-J Day and interned by the Viet Minh. An OSS outfit working with the Viet Minh refused to intervene in his behalf, and the French interpreted this refusal as distinctly anti-French.[76]

During the occupation period in north Vietnam, the French interpreted seemingly all signs of OSS cooperation with the Viet Minh as anti-French in purpose. An example was the role of the OSS in founding the Vietnamese-American Friendship Association (VAFA) on October 17, 1945. Instrumental in the founding of VAFA was Major Robert Buckley, the State Department representative with the OSS.[77] According to M. Trinh-van-Binh, the Chairman of the first meeting of the Association, the main objectives of VAFA were as follows: to get the American and Vietnamese peoples to know each other better and to cultivate friendship between them; to translate American publications into Vietnamese and Vietnamese publications into English so that the two peoples could become thoroughly acquainted with each other's culture and civilization; to organize talks and lectures in English and Vietnamese; to publish a monthly magazine in both languages; and finally

[75] Hale's Report, *op. cit.*, p. 2.
[76] Fall, *The Two Vietnams, op. cit.*, p. 41n.
[77] See Buttinger, *op. cit.*, I, 341.

to organize courses of English and Vietnamese for the members of the Association. At the inaugural meeting of VAFA, General Gallagher and several of his aides sang songs which were broadcast over the Viet Minh-controlled radio.[78] Seemingly innocuous to the Americans involved, it was occurrences such as this which led many Frenchmen to conclude that the OSS, as well as Gallagher and other Americans in Vietnam, were in reality supporting the Viet Minh.[79]

French bitterness against OSS activities in north Vietnam after V-J Day is a constant theme running throughout French writings on this period. According to Philippe Devillers, for instance, once the war was over "Americans in Vietnam assured the Viet Minh of their support." Moreover, they emphasized to the Viet Minh the advantages of breaking with France and collaborating with the United States.[80]

A similar accusation was made by Jean Sainteny. According to Sainteny, who arrived in Hanoi on the same plane as Patti's OSS group on August 22 after considerable previous harassment from General Wedemeyer,[81] he had been told by Patti that no text of Potsdam had ever mentioned French sovereignty over Indo-China and that the French no longer had a right to intervene in affairs which were no longer their concern. This prompted Sainteny to radio his superiors in Calcutta on August 28, 1945:

We are faced with a deliberate Allied maneuver to evict

---

[78] See the *VAFA Review,* November, 1945, p. 1, in the Gallagher Papers.

[79] Fall, *The Two Vietnams, op. cit.,* p. 69.

[80] Devillers, *op. cit.,* p. 152.

[81] General Wedemeyer, evidently still acting in accordance with Roosevelt's directive to give no political aid to the French in Indo-China, had at first delayed in China the departure of Sainteny, whose professed mission was to reassert French sovereignty over Indo-China as soon as possible. See Jean Sainteny, *Histoire d'une Pax Manquée* (Paris: Amiot Dumont, 1953), pp. 66–72.

the French from Indo-China. Only the Government may attempt a protest at international level. . . . It must be realized that there is no longer a French North Indo-China at the present time.

Then in early September, Sainteny observed that

The U.S. mission [under Patti] no longer bothered to conceal its hostility . . . [for] its position was very clear: warmed by the astute members of the new Annam government, swelled with pride by the importance which the French themselves attached to them, persuaded of the necessity of delivering those poor Annamites from the stranglehold of French colonialism, entirely ignorant of the related problems, not only in Indo-China but in all the Far East, the representatives of the United States, played without reserve, perhaps involuntarily, the game of Annamite nationalism. After the capitulation of the Japanese, certain U.S. services became brusquely hostile to the French. . . . [For example] a telegram from OSS was found . . . [which] stated: "In no case must the French be allowed to penetrate into Indo-China."[82]

Another accusation against the OSS was made in 1953 by Louise Villefosse, who wrote that as early as 1942 the OSS from China had tried to institute a Sino-American protectorate over Indo-China, "at least around Tonking." She then added that OSS agents in the fall of 1945 "not only openly supported the Viet Minh, but aimed to incite them against us and to sabotage the possibility of an accord."[83]

Although there is no evidence to corroborate the specifics of these French accusations against the OSS, there is evidence that the OSS did act, at least verbally, against the French and for the Viet Minh. Both General Gallagher and Colonel Nordlinger have informed this author that there

---

[82] *Ibid.*, pp. 91, 124–125.

[83] Louise Villefosse, "Les États-Unis en Indo-Chine," *Les Temps Modernes,* IX (August-September, 1953), p. 450.

was no question in their minds that Patti's activities favored the Viet Minh.[84]

There is strong denial by Gallagher and his subordinates, however, of French accusations concerning alleged political-economic anti-French activities by MAAG and the OSS during the Fall of 1945. These charges were brought up initially by General Sabattier who writes of "the odious politicking of the OSS with American capitalist groups (especially the Donovan group)."[85] These charges were levied most sharply, however, by Pierre Dessinges, a French newspaper correspondent in Vietnam after the war. In an article written for *Le Monde* in 1947, Dessinges leveled a direct charge of economic imperialism against the OSS:

> On October 15, Patti, putting his cards on the table, offered economic advantages in exchange for the independence of Vietnam, and on October 22, an American note to Ho Chi Minh defined the policy of the United States to the People's Republic [of Vietnam].

At this time, Dessinges added, General Gallagher, "the politician of the Donovan group," stepped in. Gallagher supposedly

> from the beginning of November, launched a vast spectacular political maneuver. He was seen at all the official ceremonies at the side of Ho Chi Minh, distributing rice to the natives. Wanting to force their hand, he promised to defend the Vietnam point of view in Washington by supporting a memorandum which he urged the government to prepare. No one knows what happened to this proposal. During this period, certain members of his mission realized fruitful business affairs by the sale of arms, for currency, and munitions. . . . [Yet] this beautiful harmony ended when Gallagher, unveiling his batteries, proposed to Ho Chi Minh to reconstruct, equip and extend the railways, roads and air-

---

[84] Gallagher's letter to author, January 5, 1967, and author's interview with Nordlinger, November 15, 1968.

[85] Sabattier, *op. cit.*, p. 337.

fields . . . on condition in all events that their operational use be reserved to the Donovan group. Ho Chi Minh refused. Disappointed, the General turned towards Prince Vinh Thuy, the ex-Bao Dai. The latter, who ran in the elections of January 6, was elected in Annam and seemed therefore to be able to rally the opponents of Viet Nam. Gallagher multiplied his advances toward him. . . .[86]

Dessinges thus made many serious charges against the OSS and Gallagher. But how accurate was the Frenchman's reporting? There is no evidence at all to support Dessinges' charges. According to General Gallagher, all of Dessinges' charges are false. Regarding the charge that Gallagher offered to Ho to rebuild Vietnam's railroads, etc., Gallagher explained: "I never wrote a note or verbally offered or bargained with Ho Chi Minh, . . . nor was I authorized to do so by any directive under which I was operating." Furthermore, Gallagher asserted that he had no "specific knowledge of the operational structure or objectives of the so-called Donovan group (OSS)," and that he had "no knowledge of their dealings on a national level with the French, Annamites or Japanese."[87] In short, Gallagher dismissed all charges of economic imperialism as "pure bunk!"[88] Finally, Gallagher termed Dessinges' charge concerning his relations with Bao Dai as "purely fictional," for neither he nor his headquarters "ever turned to him for anything."[89]

Several members of MAAG who worked closely with Gallagher firmly corroborated his denials. In late 1954, Gallagher sent letters to these aides requesting their views on the charges made by Dessinges. According to Colonel

---

[86] Pierre-Maurice Dessinges, "Les Intrigues Internationales en Indochine Francaise," *Le Monde,* April 13, 1947, p. 1.

[87] Letter from General Gallagher to Bernard Fall, March 30, 1956, in the Gallagher Papers.

[88] Gallagher's handwritten margin comment on Dessinges' article, in the Gallagher Papers.

[89] Gallagher's letter to Fall, *op. cit.*

John H. Stodter, who was MAAG's staff officer for intelligence matters, although Gallagher "expressed sympathy for the condition of the country [Vietnam] and recognized the need for reconstruction, no promises were made to Ho Chi Minh and no mention was made of the "Donovan Group" [sic] obtaining economic advantages." Stodter concluded that during his tour at Gallagher's headquarters, he "never heard of any promises to, or bargains with Ho Chi Minh or any other native leader."[90]

Lieutenant Reginald Ungern, General Gallagher's aide, confirmed Gallagher's denials. "This fellow Dessinges has concocted a melodramatic and untruthful hash of a tale with all sorts of fanciful implications," claimed Ungern. Furthermore, "OSS had no 'odious' policy, and especially you did not support any policy of OSS. I am quite certain that your recollection as to your relations with Patti and the OSS are correct." Ungern then added that Gallagher's recollections on Bao Dai were "completely accurate." Moreover, "for all practical purposes, Ho never knew Bao Dai existed!" And summing up, Ungern asserted:

> Your relations with Bao Dai were completely impersonal and of no significance politically. As you point out, OSS operated as a separate organization, and certainly never had your support as they were not responsible to you except insofar as regards the bare minima of military courtesy. . . .[91]

In reviewing OSS activities in North Vietnam in the period August-October 1945, there appear to be several reasons why this group of Americans supported the Viet Minh. The chief explanation may be that Patti and most of his men had worked closely with Ho during the war. They had been greatly impressed by the Viet Minh guer-

---

[90] Letter from Colonel John H. Stodter to General Gallagher, January 17, 1955, in the Gallagher Papers.
[91] Letter from Lieutenant Reginald Ungern to General Gallagher, November 26, 1954, in the Gallagher Papers.

rillas' determination and their effective resistance against the Japanese, thus many were personally sympathetic to the Viet Minh quest for independence from the French after the war. Moreover, OSS units were probably as much anti-French as pro-Vietnamese, for they had seen the sharp contrast between the bitter anti-Japanese resistance efforts of the Viet Minh and the passive submissiveness of the French.

Another explanation for the pro-Viet Minh actions of the OSS units is that they may have been utilized as a hedge on policy, leaving an option for the United States Government in case of a shift in policy requirements.

A third possibility is that the OSS men acted on their own and did not reflect American policy. This argument was supported by Lauriston Sharp, Indo-China desk officer in the Department of State in the Fall of 1945. According to Sharp, "However charmed by Ho's winning personality or prejudiced against French colonialism these OSS [men] . . . might be, it is clear that they were not spokesmen for official American policy, nor is there any evidence that they even influenced such policy."[92]

The question of control of OSS activities in Vietnam must thus be examined. General Wedemeyer asserts that when he assumed command of the China Theater, he authorized OSS operations to continue in that area. General Sultan, the American Commander in the India-Burma Theater, also authorized OSS units to remain there and operate. Wedemeyer personally told General William Donovan that although

he would be glad to have OSS troops in the China Theater, . . . their plans and operations must be undertaken in co-ordination with China Theater operations and that under

---

[92] Personal correspondence from Sharp to Bernard Fall, quoted in Bernard Fall, *The Political Development of Vietnam: V-J Day to the Geneva Cease-Fire,* Ph.D. Thesis, Syracuse University, 1954, p. 898.

no circumstances would OSS forces operate in the Theater without the knowledge and approval of the China Theater headquarters.[93]

Wedemeyer maintains that he was "theoretically in charge of OSS operations in Indo-China." Two factors, however, made Wedemeyer's control over the OSS more theoretical than real. First, although the issue of whether Indo-China military operations were to be under British or American control was never officially resolved, by the summer of 1945 Wedemeyer had accepted *de facto* the paramountcy of Mountbatten's command over that area.[94] An indication of Wedemeyer's relatively limited authority and interest in Indo-China was his reply to two personal requests from Ho Chi Minh soon after the Potsdam Conference. Ho wanted Wedemeyer to help him remain independent of French control and to expel all Frenchmen in Vietnam. Ho also was greatly concerned about the possibility of China's imperialist designs on Vietnam and asked Wedemeyer to insure that China kept a "hands off" policy toward his country. Wedemeyer disregarded Ho's first request, explaining that he could not act without definite instructions from the JCS. Concerning Ho's second request, Wedemeyer did recommend to Chiang that trouble could be avoided by minimizing the number of Chinese forces deployed in Indo-China during the occupation. Chiang agreed with Wedemeyer on this point, partly because the Kuomintang had its hands full containing the Chinese Communists at home[95]

Also inhibiting Wedemeyer's effective control over OSS operations in Vietnam was the fact that the OSS was accustomed, at times, to operating independently. According to Wedemeyer, it was for this very reason that General MacArthur refused to permit OSS operations in his theater.

---

[93] Wedemeyer's letter to author, January 19, 1967.
[94] See pp. 71–72.
[95] Wedemeyer's letter to author, January 30, 1967.

MacArthur had told Wedemeyer that he had heard that the OSS had gotten out of hand in other areas by operating independently, much to the embarrassment of the theater commander in whose area they were located. Thus Mac-Arthur had his own organization which conducted OSS-type operations in his theater. Wedemeyer, on the other hand, who personally greatly admired General Donovan, allowed OSS activities to continue in his theater. Wede-meyer admits, however, that not all OSS activities in Indo-China were known to him. Thus, Wedemeyer explains, he himself and to a greater extent General Gallagher were frequently uninformed about OSS operations in Vietnam since "it was not always feasible or possible or desirable to inform the entire command in the field concerning these [clandestine and quasi-military] operations."[96]

We can now understand why General Gallagher not only did not control OSS operations in north Vietnam but often did not even know what the OSS was doing in the area. Gallagher himself insisted that the OSS was not under his command and did not operate for him or his headquar-ters.[97] Moreover, Gallagher did not even know under whose directives the OSS did operate, and this disturbed him. "OSS always operated independently," he has remarked, "and most commanders didn't like it." And as to whether OSS operated independently from Washington, Gallagher claims he never knew. Gallagher concludes, therefore, that "OSS groups usually had considerable freedom of action and just who Patti looked to for orders is unknown to me."[98]

Although the OSS was not under Gallagher's actual con-trol, he thought that a paragraph of his directive—"to co-ordinate and supervise the activities of all other U.S. agen-cies within each command"—gave him the right to try to

---

[96] Wedemeyer's letter to author, January 19, 1967.
[97] Gallagher's letter to Fall, *op. cit.*
[98] Gallagher's letter to author, January 5, 1967.

oversee OSS operations in his command area. Gallagher appreciated the fact that Patti was able to provide both Lu Han and himself with "much valuable information" regarding Japanese papers, documents, and activities. Yet Gallagher was irritated by Patti's personal qualities and independent actions. Summarizing his views on Patti, Gallagher wrote:

> . . . Patti talks too much, and he is ingratiating to the Annamites, the French, and the Japs. He explains he does this to get all the information he wants. He has got a great deal of information, and is pretty much in the know about what is going on. . . . [On the other hand] he loves to appear mysterious, and is an alarmist. He always gets me into the corner of a room and whispers into my ear. When I enter a room, I expect to see him come out from under a rug. . . . I don't think much of him personally, believe he is trying to build up an empire and appear important.[99]

Because Patti tended to "Free wheel, resenting, not too pointedly, [Gallagher's] trying to coordinate and supervise his activities," and since Patti "tended to "muddy" up [MAAG's] effort to avoid participation in Annamese vs. French political affairs,"[100] Gallagher advised McClure to remove him "at an early date," replacing him with "someone a little less spectacular."[101] Patti was not removed, but his activities in Vietnam ceased shortly thereafter in October 1945.

What conclusions can be drawn regarding American policy and activities during the occupation period? First, declaratory United States policy opposed intervention in the struggle between the French and the Vietnamese. In effect, however, this meant support for the French since the United States was the only power in a position to aid

---

[99] Gallagher's letter to McClure, September 20, 1945. Patti has declined to comment on his role in Vietnam during this period.

[100] Gallagher's letter to author, January 5, 1967.

[101] Gallagher's letter to McClure, September 20, 1945.

the Vietnamese in their quest for independence. American action policy in Vietnam was much more complex. During the initial phase of the occupation, MAAG and G-5 generally followed their directives of August 24, 1945, to help in the surrender of the Japanese and to rehabilitate Allied prisoners, but not to become involved in political conflict between the French and the Vietnamese. By the third week of September, however, the Chinese Combat Command had issued MAAG new orders to help the Chinese reimpose French control in north Vietnam. These new orders had only a limited effect because of the reluctance of the Chinese occupation forces to comply with them. OSS units, on the other hand, continued their wartime cooperation with the Viet Minh. This cooperation caused many Frenchmen to believe that the United States Government was in actuality supporting the Vietnamese, which made France's efforts to regain control of Vietnam much more difficult. American policy in the fall of 1945, therefore, did not win the support of either the provisional Vietnamese Government or the French, but antagonized both.

It is uncertain, of course, whether the small groups of Americans in north Vietnam, had they been so directed, could have prevented a French takeover. Perhaps if Washington had considered it politically advantageous to do so, the United States could have pressed at Potsdam for a greater role in the occupation of Indo-China and could have sent a larger contingent of Americans there after the war to make a greater effort to influence policy. Vietnam, however, was of very low priority to Washington politically and thus the Americans in north Vietnam after the war were given very little direction and wherewithal to effect any significant policy developments.

CONCLUSION

United States policy toward Vietnam in the period 1940 to 1945 can be understood only in terms of its global setting. Until the Japanese began their aggressive march into Southeast Asia and stationed forces in Vietnam, the United States had virtually no policy toward this far off French colony. But when President Roosevelt decided that Japanese occupation of Indo-China in 1940-1941 posed a direct threat to the Philippines and United States interests in the Pacific, the area suddenly assumed tremendous strategic significance. The United States warned the Japanese that it could not tolerate this situation and that force would be used if necessary to ensure their withdrawal.

After the Japanese attack on Pearl Harbor and the American entry into the war in Asia, the strategic importance of Indo-China to the United States diminished considerably for the French colony was virtually bypassed in Allied military strategy against Japan. Indo-China, however, began to assume great political importance to the United States. In the early stages of the war, the formulation of American policy toward Indo-China was complicated by the problem of the two competing sets of French authorities, the Vichy Government and the Free French. The United States maintained diplomatic recognition of the Vichy regime until the summer of 1944 because this was considered the most effective way to prevent the French from further aiding the German war effort and to mobilize French resistance against the Axis powers wherever and whenever possible.

One of Vichy's main aims was to enlist military assistance from the United States to thwart Japanese advances in Indo-China. In pursuit of this aim, representatives of Vichy made frequent remonstrations in Washington. Despite the frequency and sense of urgency of Vichy's pleas, the United States steadfastly declined to send any military aid. Although this refusal caused considerable friction between Vichy and Washington, the United States argued that it could offer no aid because the French in Indo-China were putting up only minimal resistance to the Japanese and because the Vichy Government, moreover, had failed to keep Washington informed on its concessions to Japan. Whether American military aid to the French in Indo-China could have prevented Japanese occupation is doubtful, especially since a large number of French there decided to collaborate with the Japanese. It can be argued that collaboration was the most logical choice in view of the lack of arms for resistance. It can also be argued, however, that collaboration was decided upon as the best way of ensuring preservation of French control over Indo-China after the war.

Indeed, a principal objective of Vichy throughout the war was to gain Washington's support for the maintenance of the French Empire. In order to increase its chances of influencing Vichy, in the early years of the war Washington gave the French Government private assurances of support for the preservation of French colonialism. The French clung tenaciously to these assurances and became increasingly distressed as the United States Government issued public pronouncements, such as the Atlantic Charter, which indicated its opposition to the continuation of colonialism after the war.

As the war progressed, the strong anticolonialism of President Roosevelt became increasingly predominant. Roosevelt began to insist that France, as well as the other European colonial powers, should follow the example set by the United States in the Philippines and begin to prepare all colonies for self-government and eventual independence. Roosevelt's desire that Indo-China not be returned to France after the war, but instead be administered by some form of international trusteeship, was a reflection of his strong opposition to colonialism everywhere. Roosevelt was convinced that colonialism had been an underlying cause of the war in the Pacific. He was particularly distressed by what he considered France's misrule in Indo-China. Thus the elimination of colonialism, especially France's rule in Indo-China, became a cardinal aim of Roosevelt's foreign policy.

France and Britain, however, were equally insistent that Indo-China remain under French control because they feared the effects that independence or a trusteeship there would have throughout their empires. A serious controversy thus arose over the postwar status of Indo-China. This controversy was accentuated by Roosevelt's attempts to restrict French and British military operations in Indo-China. Roosevelt hoped thereby to minimize French and British political influence in Indo-China after the war. The President was only partly successful in these attempts. In the later stages of the war when the French were anxious to land troops in Indo-China to "liberate" their colony from the Japanese, the United States indeed faced with an actual shipping shortage, refused to urge the Allied Shipping Commission to provide the French with the necessary shipping. Moreover, the United States offered very limited assistance to French resistance groups in Indo-China, which had organized only as late as the end of 1944 when the defeat of the Axis powers seemed imminent. These policy decisions especially infuriated Charles de Gaulle, who considered them additional evidence of Roosevelt's disdain for him and his Free French movement. On the other hand, Roosevelt was unsuccessful in restricting British control over military operations in Indo-China. After a long dis-

pute between General Wedemeyer and Admiral Mountbatten as to whose theater command Indo-China fell under,
the British position prevailed. By the end of the war, Indo-
China was considered under the British Southeast Asia
Command. At the Potsdam Conference in July-August
1945, therefore, the British were given occupation responsibility in southern Indo-China and the Americans
were given only an advisory role to the Chinese occupation
forces in the north. Regardless of the outcome of this
theater dispute, the United States probably would not
have sent occupation troops into any part of Indo-China
nor into any other European colonies in Asia. Such actions
not only would have called for the deployment of large
numbers of U. S. forces, which would have been virtually
impossible in the face of congressional and public pressure
for rapid postwar demobilization, but also would have
seemed both unnecessary and undesirable in light of Washington's decision near the end of the war not to oppose
the reestablishment of control by our European allies over
their Asian colonies.

When the Big Three began to formulate firm plans for
the postwar world, President Roosevelt felt compelled to
drop his international trusteeship plan for Indo-China.
The turning point came in June-August 1944. The invasion of France in June and Roosevelt's recognition of
the French Committee of National Liberation as the "dominant" political authority in France during de Gaulle's
visit to Washington in July provided the background for
Roosevelt's decision at Dumbarton Oaks in August. At
this conference, Washington conceded that Indo-China
would be placed under trusteeship only with the permis-
sion of France, which was highly improbable. The decision grew out of the "Europe first" military strategy. Roosevelt decided that military cooperation with Britain and
France required a measure of political cooperation which

was considered more important than support for the independence of Indo-China. Roosevelt's decision also may have been influenced by de Gaulle's promises to grant Indo-China a greater measure of self-government after the war.

President Truman also based his Indo-China policy on these premises. For Truman, however, the considerations were somewhat different in the summer of 1945 from what they had been for Roosevelt the previous summer. Truman was also sympathetic toward the independence of Indo-China, but after the war he felt it was more important for the United States to work for a stable French Government which would oppose possible Soviet encroachments in Western Europe.

After the Viet Minh established the Provisional Government of Vietnam on August 20, 1945, and declared an independent Vietnam on September 2, official American policy toward this regime at first was political noninvolvement. In accordance with this policy, the United States did not recognize the Vietnam Government. Moreover, Washington said that it would not interfere in any conflict between European colonial powers and their colonies. The groups of Americans sent to north Vietnam to help the Chinese with their occupation duties and to rehabilitate Allied prisoners of war were thus instructed not to become involved in political conflicts between the French and the Vietnamese. The neutrality of these Americans was strained, however, because all major groups in Vietnam, both native and foreign, expected the United States to help them achieve their aims. The French expected the Americans to help them gain control of north Vietnam just as the British had helped them retake south Vietnam. The Chinese looked to the Americans, particularly the Military Advisory and Assistance Group, for advice and aid in executing their occupation duties. And the Viet Minh leaders sought help from the Americans to achieve independence.

Indeed, Ho Chi Minh looked mainly to the United States as the country most able and willing to assist his regime against the French.

By the third week in September 1945, the pressures in the United States for rapid troop demobilization and the requirements of a "Europe first" policy led to the American decision to try to facilitate the reimposition of French control in Vietnam through the efforts of MAAG. The French were overjoyed, and the Viet Minh leaders were dismayed. The efforts of MAAG to help the French politically were stymied by Lu Han, the leader of the Chinese occupation forces, who refused to aid the French regain political control. As a result, whatever aid MAAG gave to the French was essentially humanitarian rather than political. The American Military Government Group also gave humanitarian aid to the French, particularly French prisoners of war. The Office of Strategic Services, however, continued its war-time policy of supporting the Viet Minh. During the war, OSS men had worked closely with Ho Chi Minh and his Viet Minh guerrillas in resistance efforts against the Japanese. They were aware of Ho's Communist background but they were impressed more by his fanatic desire to gain independence for Vietnam. Possibly the OSS was acting on its own, or possibly it was a hedge on policy in case Washington's policy requirements shifted. Whatever the case, many Frenchmen interpreted OSS activities in Vietnam as evidence that the United States Government was in actuality working against France and was trying to establish American control over Vietnam. The Viet Minh, on the other hand, hoped that OSS sympathy for its cause would lead to United States Government support for Vietnam's independence effort. OSS activity was short-lived, for it ceased operations in October, 1945. In the immediate postwar period, therefore, both the French and the Viet Minh believed that the Americans betrayed their cause because neither received the political support from the Americans which they expected.

One of the most serious criticisms that has been directed against American policy toward Vietnam at the end of World War II was its failure to support the Viet Minh quest for independence. In retrospect, this was one of the most important failures in American diplomatic history. This failure, however, should be attributed not to hypocrisy but to the prevailing concept of U.S. national interest. After the war, the United States placed a higher priority on cooperation with Britain and France in Europe than on independence for Vietnam. As a result, Vietnam was virtually lost in the postwar shuffle of events and the United States began to stumble into a course of backing French colonialism.

BIBLIOGRAPHY

Unpublished Primary Sources

Army Files, United States Government

French Indochina, Book I, China Theater Files. World War II
Reference Branch, Alexandria, Virginia. Author unknown.

> Contains valuable documentary material. Recently de-
> classified.

History of U. S. Forces in China Theater. MS in Office of the
Chief of Military History. Washington, D. C. Author unknown.

> Reveals the political as well as the military role of the
> United States Army.

Papers of General Philip E. Gallagher, in Office of the Chief
of Military History.

> An extremely valuable collection of official U. S. Gov-
> ernment documents, letters, and memoranda by the senior
> American military commander in north Vietnam during
> the fall of 1945.
>
> Of special importance is the report of Arthur Hale.
> Hale was a representative of the U. S. Information Agency
> who based his report concerning conditions in northern
> Vietnam upon a stay of thirteen days in Hanoi from Oc-
> tober 15 through October 28, 1945, and upon conversa-
> tions with American officers who came out of northern
> Vietnam later.

Collection of Ambassador Papers

The Patrick J. Hurley Collection, in University of Oklahoma,
Norman, Oklahoma.

167

Contains many important exchanges between Ambassador Hurley and Washington regarding plans for the postwar future of China and European colonies in Southeast Asia.

Conference

U. S. Department of State. Conference on Problems of United States Policy in China. October 6–8, 1949.

This conference, originally classified *Confidential,* is an important record of statements and opinions of Governmental officials and academic experts on Asia.

Interviews by author

Edmund Gullion, former U.S. Deputy Minister to the Associated States of Indo-China and now Dean of the Fletcher School of Law and Diplomacy. December 11, 1966.

Jean Lacouture, French journalist and author. June 7, 1966.

S. L. Nordlinger, Colonel in U.S. Army in charge of Military Government (G-5) in north Vietnam in the fall of 1945. February 16, 1967, November 15, 1968.

Waldron C. White, American Red Cross representative in Hanoi in the fall of 1945. November 29, 1968.

Letters to author

Everett Case, special consultant on Far Eastern Affairs to Secretary of State Dean Acheson, 1949. January 17, 1966.

Philip E. Gallagher, General in U.S. Army in charge of U.S. MAAG in north Vietnam in the fall of 1945. January 5, 1967, January 10, 1969.

Donald Heath, first U.S. Minister and Ambassador to the Associated States of Indo-China, 1950-1954. February 11, 1966.

John Melby, Chairman of joint State-Defense Military Assistance Aid Mission to Southeast Asia, July, 1950. January 18, 1966, January 26, 1966.

S. L. Nordlinger. February 6, 1967.

Albert C. Wedemeyer, U.S. General who was chief of staff and military adviser to Chiang Kai-shek during World War II. January 19, 1967, January 30, 1967.

Published Primary Sources

Documents

Cole, Allan B. (ed.). *Conflict in Indo-China and International Repercussions, A Documentary History, 1945-1955*. Ithaca, N. Y.: Cornell University Press, 1956.

An important collection of documents by an American scholar on the France-Indo-China conflict. Contains short introductions to main aspects of the war, and a valuable chronology of events.

Great Britain. *Documents Relating to British Involvement in the Indo-China Conflict, 1945-1965*. H.M.S.O., Cmd. 2834. December, 1965.

A documentary history of Britain's involvement in the Indo-China War, with editorial comments. Also valuable for Britain's assessment of the roles played by major powers in the conflict.

Rathausky, Rima (ed.). *Documents of the August 1945 Revolution*. Canberra: The Australian National University, 1963.

Contains important documents of the Viet Minh and the Communist Party of Indo-China.

U.S. *Department of State Bulletin*, 1940-1946, *passim*.

U.S. Department of State, *Foreign Relations of the United States, Diplomatic Papers 1940, The Far East*. Washington: Government Printing Office, 1955.

U.S. Department of State. *Foreign Relations of the United States, Diplomatic Papers 1941, Europe*. Washington: Government Printing Office, 1959.

————. *Foreign Relations of the United States, Diplomatic Papers 1943, China*. Washington: Government Printing Office, 1957.

————. *Foreign Relations of the United States, Diplomatic Papers 1943, The Conferences at Cairo and Tehran*. Washington: Government Printing Office, 1961.

————. *Foreign Relations of the United States, Diplomatic Papers 1944, The British Commonwealth and Europe*. Washington: Government Printing Office, 1965.

————. *Foreign Relations of the United States, Diplomatic Papers 1945, The Conference of Berlin.* Washington: Government Printing Office, 1960.

————. *Foreign Relations of the United States, Diplomatic Papers 1945, The Conferences at Malta.* Washington: Government Printing Office, 1955.

————. *Foreign Relations of the United States, Diplomatic Papers 1945, General: The United Nations.* Washington: Government Printing Office, 1967.

————. *Papers Relating to the Foreign Relations of the United States, Japan: 1931-1941.* 2 vols. Washington: Government Printing Office, 1943.

————. *Peace and War: United States Foreign Policy, 1931-1941.* Washington: Government Printing Office, 1943.

The Foreign Relations series is an invaluable source of official documents on American foreign policy.

————. *United States Relations with China.* Washington: Government Printing Office, 1949.

Contains an appendix of important documents with relevance to Vietnam.

U.S. Department of State. Office of Intelligence Research, Division of Research for Far East. *Political Alignments of Vietnamese Nationalists.* OIR Report No. 3708. October 1, 1949.

An assessment of the role of Ho Chi Minh, the Viet Minh, and the Communist Party of Indo-China in the Indo-China conflict.

U.S. Office of Strategic Services, Research and Analysis Branch. *Program of Geographic Work Fundamental to Far East Problems.* R&A No. 3315. August 18, 1945.

Reveals the low priority of Vietnam in America's postwar plans.

————. *Programs of Japan in Indochina.* Honolulu, August 10, 1945.

Declassified F.C.C. intercepts of shortwave broadcasts (except those of a purely military nature) from Radio Tokyo and affiliated stations from December 1941 to May 24, 1945, and compilations from OSS sources. Indispensable for understanding developments in Indo-China during the war.

U.S. Senate. Committee on Armed Services and the Committee on Foreign Relations. *Hearings on the Military Situation in the Far East.* 82d Cong., 1st Sess., Parts 1 and 4, 1951.

————. Committee on Foreign Relations. *Testimony by Edwin Reischauer, Asia, the Pacific, and the United States.* 9th Cong., 1st Sess., 1967.

————. Subcommittee of the Committee on the Judiciary. *Hearings on the Institute of Pacific Relations.* 82d Cong., Part 13, 1952.

These hearings contain significant documents and testimony regarding United States Far East and Southeast Asia Policy.

Memoirs and Biographies

Chennault, Claire L. *Way of a Fighter.* New York: G. P. Putnam's Sons, 1949.

Memoirs of the famous leader of the "Flying Tigers" and commander of the 14th United States Air Force in Yunnan during World War II.

Churchill, Winston. *The Second World War.* 6 vols. New York: Bantam, 1962.

Especially interesting for the author's assessment of United States policy during the war.

Decoux, Jean. *A La Barre de L'Indochine: Histoire de mon Gouvernement Général, 1940-1945.* Paris: Plon, 1949.

The Admiral-Governor General's defense of his policy of collaboration with the Japanese.

Eden, Anthony. *Full Circle.* Cambridge, Mass.: Houghton Mifflin, 1960.

Contains good insights into American as well as British policy.

Forrestal, James. *The Forrestal Diaries.* New York: Viking, 1951.

The memoirs of an astute American statesman.

de Gaulle, Charles. *War Memoirs: Salvation, 1944-1946, Documents.* Translated by Joyce Murchie and Hamish Erskine. New York: Simon & Schuster, 1960.

————. *The War Memoirs of Charles de Gaulle, Salvation, 1944-1946*. Translated by Richard Howard. New York: Simon & Schuster, 1967.

Grew, Joseph C. *Ten Years in Japan*. New York: Simon & Schuster, 1944.

The American Ambassador to Japan at the time of Pearl Harbor analyzes American-Japanese relations leading to the attack.

Hull, Cordell. *The Memoirs of Cordell Hull*. 2 vols. New York: Macmillan Co., 1948.

The American Secretary of State reviews United States diplomacy during World War II.

Leahy, William. *I Was There*. New York: McGraw Hill, 1950.

The personal wartime experiences of the United States Ambassador to Vichy.

Lohbeck, Don. *Patrick J. Hurley*. Chicago: Henry Regenry, 1956 .

The official biography of the United States Ambassador to China in the late war years.

Mus, Paul. "L'Indochine en 1945," *Politique Étrangère*, XI (August, 1946) , 349-374, 433-464.

Roosevelt, Elliott. *As He Saw It*. New York: Duell, Sloane & Pearce, 1945.

President Roosevelt's son recalls his father's views and actions.

Sabattier, G. *Le Destin de l'Indochine, Souvenirs et Documents (1941-1951)*. Paris: Plon, 1952.

The French General in charge of French troops in Tongking analyzes the role of the French military during the Japanese occupation of Indo-China. Contains a valuable collection of documents.

Sainteny, Jean. *Histoire d'une Pax Manquée*. Paris: Aimot Dumont, 1953.

The reminiscences of the first representative of de Gaulle's provisional French Government to enter north Vietnam after the defeat of the Japanese. Very critical of United States policy in north Vietnam after V-J Day.

Stettinius, Edward, Jr. *Roosevelt and the Russians*. Garden City: Doubleday, 1949.

Observations on Roosevelt's policies by the Under Secretary of State who became Secretary of State near the end of the war.

Truman, Harry S. *Memoirs.* 2 vols. New York: Signet, 1965.

Wedemeyer, Albert C. *Wedemeyer Reports!* New York: Holt, Reinhart and Winston, 1958.

The impressions of the American General in charge of China theater operations sent after the war to assess the chaotic situation in China.

Newspapers

New York Times, 1940-1945, *passim.*

Le Monde, 1940-1945, *passim.*

Secondary Sources

Unpublished Dissertations

Dunn, William B. "American Policy and Vietnamese Nationalism, 1950-1954." University of Chicago, 1960.

A superficial examination of the United States attempt to cope with Vietnamese nationalism since World War II.

Fall, Bernard. "Political Development of Vietnam, V-J Day to the Geneva Cease-Fire." Syracuse University, 1954.

A very detailed and incisive study.

Official Studies

Donnison, F. S. V. *British Military Administration in the Far East, 1943-1946. London:* Her Majesty's Stationery Office, 1956.

Matloff, Maurice. *Strategic Planning for Coalition Warfare, 1943-1944.* Washington: Department of the Army, 1959.

Morton, Louis. *Strategy and Command: The First Two Years.* Washington: Department of the Army, 1962.

Notter, Harley A. (ed.). *Postwar Foreign Policy Preparation, 1939-1945.* Department of State Publication 3580. Washington: Government Printing Office, 1950.

Romanus, Charles F., and Riley Sunderland. *Time Runs Out in CBI*. Washington: Department of the Army, 1959.

Sparrow, John C. *History of Personnel Demobilization in the United States Army*. Washington: Department of the Army, 1951.

Vigneras, Marcel. *United States Army in World War II, Special Studies, Rearming the French*. Washington: Department of the Army, 1957.

Woodward, Llewellyn. *British Foreign Policy in the Second World War*. London: Her Majesty's Stationery Office, 1962.

These are well-documented, government-sponsored research studies.

Books

Asher, Robert, *et al*. *The United Nations and Promotion of the General Welfare*. Washington: The Brookings Institute, 1957. A useful collection of essays.

Bodard, Lucien. *La Guerre d'Indochine, l'Enlisement*. Paris: Gallimard, 1963.

A rather superficial account of the Indo-China War.

Butow, Robert C. *Tojo and the Coming of the War*. Princeton, N. J.: Princeton University Press, 1961.

A well-documented analysis of events leading to the Japanese attack on Pearl Harbor.

Buttinger, Joseph. *Vietnam: A Dragon Embattled*. 2 vols. New York: Praeger, 1967.

The most exhaustive study of Vietnam to date. Discusses the turbulent history of Vietnam from virtually every point of view, focusing on the years 1900 to 1963.

Cooper, Bert, *et al*. *Case Studies in Insurgency and Revolutionary Warfare: Vietnam, 1941-1954*. Washington: The American University, 1964.

A well-researched study on Vietnam's insurgency. Particularly important for its treatment of American policy.

Dean, Vera Micheles. *Main Trends in Postwar American Foreign Policy*. New Delhi: Oxford University Press, 1950.

A scholar's review of America's postwar policy dilemmas.

Despuetch, Jacques. *Le Traffic de Piastres*. Paris: Deux Rives, 1953.

A rather sensationalist exposé of the Piastre scandals during the Indo-China war.

Devillers, Philippe. *Histoire du Vietnam de 1940 à 1952*. Paris: Editions du Seuil, 1952.

An extensive analysis by a noted French scholar of French policy in Vietnam during thirteen critical years. The tone is distinctly anti-American.

Elgey, Georgette. *La Republique des Illusions, 1945-1951*. Paris: Fayard, 1965.

A critical account of French attempts to regain control of Vietnam after World War II.

Fall, Bernard (ed.). *Ho Chi Minh on Revolution*. New York: Praeger, 1967.

A valuable collection of Ho's speeches and writings by one of America's leading authorities on Vietnam.

———. *The Two Vietnams*. New York: Praeger, 1967.

A well-documented history of North and South Vietnam. Well-balanced and informative.

Farley, Miriam S. *United States Relations with Southeast Asia*. New York: Institute of Pacific Relations, 1955.

A brief but well-documented analysis of America's post-war policy in Southeast Asia.

Feis, Herbert. *Churchill, Roosevelt, and Stalin*. Princeton: Princeton University Press, 1957.

An important study of the wartime relations of the "Big Three."

———. *The China Tangle*. New York: Atheneum, 1965.

A very well-researched study by an American historian of American attempts to formulate a China policy during and immediately after World War II.

———. *The Road to Pearl Harbor*. New York: Atheneum, 1965.

An excellent analysis of the events leading to Japan's attack.

Finkelstein, Lawrence S. *American Policy in Southeast Asia*. New York: Institute of Pacific Relations, 1950.

A balanced review of America's postwar policy in Southeast Asia after World War II.

Furniss, Edgar S., Jr. *France: Keystone of Western Defense.* Garden City: Doubleday, 1954.

An analysis of France's role in the defense of western Europe after World War II.

Gaudel, André. *L'Indochine Francaise en face du Japon.* Paris: J. Susse, 1947.

A survey of economic, military, and political problems of Indo-China between 1939 and 1945.

Hammer, Ellen J. *The Struggle for Indochina.* Stanford: Stanford University Press, 1966.

An authoritative analysis of French policy during the Indo-China war. Well-documented and balanced.

Henderson, William (ed.). *Southeast Asia: Problems of United States Policy.* Cambridge, Mass.: M.I.T. Press, 1963.

Contains many informative essays.

Hertrich, Jean-Michel. *Doc-Lap! L'indépendance ou la Mort.* Paris: Vigneau, 1946.

A Frenchman's impressions of the Viet Minh's struggle for independence in August 1945.

Holland, William L. (ed.). *Asian Nationalism and the West.* New York: Macmillan, 1953.

A useful collection of essays.

Horton, Mildred M. (ed.). *America's Failure in the Pacific.* New Brunswick, N.J.: Rutgers University Press, 1947.

A compilation of lectures given by U.S. Government officials at Wellesley College in October 1946.

Hytier, Adrienne. *Two Years of French Foreign Policy, Vichy 1940-1942.* Paris: Librairie Minard, 1958.

A pro-French account, critical of United States policy toward Vichy.

Isaacs, Harold R. *No Peace for Asia.* New York: Macmillan, 1947.

An eyewitness account of developments in Vietnam in 1945-1946 (pp. 134-176) by the Asian correspondent of *Newsweek.* Very critical of the United States and sympathetic to the Vietnamese quest for independence.

Kelley, George A. *Lost Soldiers.* Cambridge, Mass.: M.I.T. Press, 1965.

A well-documented study by a young American scholar

on the role of the French army in French colonial wars after 1945.

Kennan, George F. *Realities of American Foreign Policy.* Princeton, N.J.: Princeton University Press, 1954.

An essay on the dilemmas of United States foreign policy after World War II.

Lacouture, Jean. *Ho Chi Minh.* New York: Random House, 1968.

A biography by the renowned foreign correspondent of *Le Monde* who has spent much time in Vietnam since World War II.

Langer, William. *Our Vichy Gamble.* New York: Norton, 1966.

An authoritative, well-documented study by a distinguished American historian on United States relations with Vichy France during the early years of World War II.

Lattimore, Owen. *Solution in Asia.* Boston: Little, Brown and Co., 1945.

A noted American scholar and government expert analyzes the opportunities for American policy in Asia after World War II.

Lippmann, Walter. *The Cold War: A Study in U.S. Foreign Policy.* New York: Harper, 1947.

A collection of articles criticizing United States policy toward Russia after World War II.

McLane, Charles B. *Soviet Strategies in Southeast Asia.* Princeton, N.J.: Princeton University Press, 1966.

A very scholarly analysis of Soviet policy in Southeast Asia based on an exhaustive review of Soviet sources.

Mende, Tibor. *Southeast Asia between the Two Worlds.* London: Turnstile Press, 1955.

A useful analysis of the problems of Southeast Asia after World War II.

Morison, Samuel Eliot. *History of United States Naval Operations in World War II, vol. III: The Rising Sun in the Pacific, 1943-April 1942.* Boston: Little Brown, 1948.

A scholarly study of American naval history.

Paillat, Claude. *Dossier Secret De l'Indochine.* Paris: Presses de la Cité, 1964.

A sensationalist account of French scandals during the Indo-China War.

Pendar, Kenneth. *Adventures in Diplomacy*. New York: Dodd, Mead, 1945.

A sketchy review of American diplomacy during World War II.

Rieber, Alfred J. *Stalin and the French Communist Party, 1941-1947*. New York: Columbia University Press, 1962.

A scholarly review of Stalin's efforts to control the French Communist party.

Russell, Ruth B. *A History of the United Nations Charter, The Role of the United States, 1940-1945*. Washington: The Brookings Institute, 1958.

A comprehensive study of the efforts by the United States to establish a united nations organization.

Schroeder, Paul. *The Axis Alliance and Japanese-American Relations 1941*. Ithaca, N.Y.: Cornell University Press, 1958.

A critical review of United States policy in the period before the attack on Pearl Harbor.

Shaplen, Robert. *The Lost Revolution*. New York: Harper and Row, 1965.

A critical account of United States policy in Vietnam since 1945 by an American correspondent with considerable experience in Vietnam.

Strausz-Hupé, Robert, and Hazard, Harry W. (eds.). *The Idea of Colonialism*. New York: Praeger, 1958.

A valuable collection of scholarly essays.

Talbot, Philip (ed.). *South Asia in the World Today*. Chicago: University of Chicago Press, 1950.

An important collection of articles on Asia's problems.

Thompson, Virginia, and Richard Adloff. *The Left Wing in Southeast Asia*. New York: Sloane, 1950.

An important study of left wing movements in Southeast Asia after World War II. Contains a valuable analysis of the rise of the Viet Minh.

Viorst, Milton. *Hostile Allies: FDR and Charles de Gaulle*. New York: Macmillan, 1965.

An informative study of the difficult relationship between Roosevelt and de Gaulle during World War II.

Wolfers, Arnold (ed.). *Alliance Policy in the Cold War*. Baltimore: Johns Hopkins Press, 1959.

Very valuable for an understanding of alliance problems since World War II.

Wright, Quincy (ed.). *A Foreign Policy for the United States*. Chicago: University of Chicago Press, 1947.

A useful collection of essays by governmental and academic experts on United States foreign policy.

Articles

Bell, Philip W. "Colonialism as a Problem in American Foreign Policy," *World Politics*, V (October, 1952), 86-109.

A scholarly analysis of the American colonialism problem in historical perspective.

Berle, Adolf A., Jr. "Our Asian Policy," *The Annals of the American Academy of Political and Social Sciences*, CCLXXVI (July, 1951), 60-71.

A government and academic expert reviews the difficulties faced by the United States in formulating an Asian policy after World War II.

Bourdet, Claude. "Les Hommes De La Guerre," *Les Temps Modernes*, IX (August-September, 1953), 401-425.

A Frenchman critically analyzes leading figures in the Indo-China war.

Cady, John F. "The Historical Background of United States Policy in Southeast Asia," in William Henderson (ed.). *Southeast Asia, Problems of United States Policy*, 1-26.

An important analytical essay.

Dessinges, Pierre M. "Les Intrigues Internationales en Indochine Francaise," *Le Monde*, April 13, 1947.

A very critical account of American policy in Vietnam in the Fall of 1945.

Dulles, Foster Rhea, and Gerald E. Ridinger. "The Anti-Colonial Policies of Franklin D. Roosevelt," *Political Science Quarterly*, LXX (March, 1955), 1-18.

A lucid, scholarly discussion.

Esthus, Raymond A. "President Roosevelt's Commitment to Britain to Intervene in a Pacific War," *The Mississippi Valley Historical Review*, L (June, 1963) , 28-38.

Fall, Bernard. "La Politique Américain du Viet-Nam," *Politique Étrangère*, XX (July, 1955), 299-322.

> One of the first accounts of American postwar policy in Vietnam.

————. "Tribulations of a Party Line, The French Communists and Indochina," *Foreign Affairs*, XXXIII (April, 1955) , 499-510.

> Shows the difficulties faced by the Soviet Union and the French Communist Party in reconciling their postwar policy priorities with the nationalist aspirations of the Communist Party of Indo-China.

Gilchrist, Huntington. "Colonial Questions at the San Francisco Conference," *American Political Science Review*, XXXIX (October, 1945) , 982-992.

Good, Robert C. "The United States and the Colonial Debate," in Arnold Wolfers (ed.) , *Alliance Policy in the Cold War*, 224-270.

> The author argues that the United States choice of backing the European colonial powers after World War II was based mainly on considerations of American national security.

Haas, Ernest B. "The Attempt to Terminate Colonialism: Acceptance of the United Nations Trusteeship System," *International Organization*, VII (February, 1953) , 1-21.

> An excellent summation of the difficulties of the Allies in reaching a mutually satisfactory agreement on the postwar status of colonies.

Henderson, William. "United States Policy and Colonialism," *Academy of Political Science, Proceedings*, XXVI (May, 1957) , 53-63.

> An analysis of the United States effort to resolve an apparent discrepancy between its professed anti-colonialism and support for European colonial powers after the war.

Isaacs, Harold R. "South Asia's Opportunity," *Modern Review*, LXXXII (December, 1947), 444-450.

A very critical analysis of America's postwar policy in Asia.

Laurel, Robert. "The Indochina Dilemma: An American Responsibility," *American Perspective*, II (June, 1948), 121-126. •

A plea for the United States to use its influence to stop the Indo-China war.

Rosinger, Lawrence K. "Wallace Outlines Basis for Post-War Harmony in Far East," *Foreign Policy Bulletin*, XXIII (June 30, 1944), 2-3.

————. "What Stand Will U.S. Take on Future of Colonial Asia?" *Foreign Policy Bulletin*, XXIV (June 22, 1945), 2-3.

The author points out the difficulties the United States was about to face in reconciling anti-Colonialism with postwar policy priorities.

Rueff, Gaston. "The Future of French Indo-China," *Foreign Affairs*, XXIII (October, 1944), 140-146.

A plea for the postwar preservation of the French empire by a member of the French Colonial Institute.

Snow, Edgar. "No Four Freedoms for Indo-China," *Saturday Evening Post*, CCXVIII (February 2, 1946), 20.

The author, sympathetic to the Vietnamese quest for independence, points out what he considers the glaring discrepancies between the professed American ideals of freedom and independence and the practice of American diplomacy in Indo-China after World War II.

Trager, Frank N. "American Foreign Policy in Southeast Asia," in Robert K. Sakai (ed.). *Studies on Asia*, 1965, 17-59.

The author criticizes the "ambivalence and uncertainty" in American postwar policy toward colonialism.

Villefosee, Louise. "Les États-Unis en Indochine," *Les Temps Modernes*, IX (August-September, 1953), 447-457.

A critical account of United States policy.

Vinacke, Harold M. "United States Far Eastern Policy," *Pacific Affairs*, XIX (December, 1946), 351-363.

A well-balanced analysis of the difficulties faced by the United States in postwar Asia.

Viner, Jacob. "The American Interest in the Colonial Problem," in Jacob Viner, *et al. The United States in a Multi-National Economy*. New York: Council on Foreign Relations, 1945.

A discussion of economic considerations in America's postwar policy decisions regarding colonialism.

INDEX